Investigative Journalism in the United States

Edd Applegate

Investigative Journalism in the United States

A History, with Profiles of Journalists and Writers Who Practiced the Form

PETER LANG
Lausanne • Berlin • Bruxelles • Chennai • New York • Oxford

Library of Congress Cataloging-in-Publication Data

Names: Applegate, Edd, author.
Title: Investigative journalism in the United States: a history, with profiles of journalists and writers who practiced the form / Edd Applegate.
Description: New York: Peter Lang, [2023] | Includes bibliographical references and index.
Identifiers: LCCN 2023019167 (print) | LCCN 2023019168 (ebook) | ISBN 9781433194771 (hardback) | ISBN 9781433194788 (ebook) | ISBN 9781433194795 (epub)
Subjects: LCSH: Investigative reporting–United States. | Journalists–United States–Biography.
Classification: LCC PN4888.I56 A67 2023 (print) | LCC PN4888.I56 (ebook) | DDC 070.92/2 [B]–dc23/eng/20230727
LC record available at https://lccn.loc.gov/2023019167
LC ebook record available at https://lccn.loc.gov/2023019168
DOI 10.3726/b19295

Bibliographic information published by the Deutsche Nationalbibliothek. The German National Library lists this publication in the German National Bibliography; detailed bibliographic data is available on the Internet at http://dnb.d-nb.de

Cover design by Peter Lang Group AG

ISBN 9781433194771 (hardback)
ISBN 9781433194788 (ebook)
ISBN 9781433194795 (epub)
DOI 10.3726/b19295

Published by Peter Lang Publishing Inc., New York, USA
info@peterlang.com - www.peterlang.com

CONTENTS

INTRODUCTION

This book discusses the history of investigative journalism in the United States and then presents the lives of journalists and writers who practiced the form during their professional careers.

Part I defines investigative journalism and examines how it evolved from the earliest years of the nation to today.

Part II discusses the lives of various journalists and writers who wrote primarily investigative journalism during their professional careers. Although coverage is heaviest of investigative journalists and writers who worked during the last seventy-five years, important writers from earlier times are included as well. The journalists and writers included in this book have been identified by more than one source as having written investigative journalism. Several of these writers have been identified as muckraking journalists, too, primarily because of what they focused on and how they wrote. For instance, a few editorialized or provided their own opinions in addition to factual information in their articles and/or books.

Each biographical sketch begins with the journalist's name and dates of birth and death, if deceased. Then the writer's life is summarized chronologically, with information pertaining to his or her professional career and major works. In a few cases, comments by others about the journalist's work have been included. Readers interested in learning more about a writer should begin with that person's works listed at the end of that person's entry as well as the sources listed under "Further Reading." The "Selected Bibliography" at the end of the book will help, too.

Part I

A History of Investigative Journalism in the United States

Investigative journalism, which has been termed adversarial journalism, exposé journalism, muckraking journalism, public service journalism, watchdog journalism, yellow journalism, to mention several, has played an important role in the United States. For instance, it has helped people learn about misconduct and corruption by politicians and businesses. It has helped break up political rings typically controlled by one or two unscrupulous individuals who had a stranglehold on a party in a city or a state or both.

What Is Investigative Journalism?

In *Story-Based Inquiry: A Manual for Investigative Journalists*, which was written by Mark Lee Hunter and others for UNESCO, "investigative journalism involves exposing to the public matters that are concealed—either deliberately by someone in a position of power, or accidentally, behind a chaotic mass of facts and circumstances that obscure understanding."[1]

Of course, there are other definitions, too, including the following:

> Investigative journalism is a form of journalism in which reporters deeply investigate a single topic of interest, such as serious crimes, political corruption, or corporate wrongdoing.[2]

According to David E. Kaplan, the executive director of the Global Investigative Journalism Network, an association of more than two hundred nonprofit groups in more than eighty countries that support investigative reporting, investigative journalism's major components are: "systematic, in-depth, and original research and reporting, often involving the unearthing of secrets."[3]

In other words, reporters who are engaged in investigative journalism often have to use public records as well as other materials they have uncovered in order to write a story or a series of stories about a specific problem.

1 Mark Lee Hunter et al., *Story-Based Inquiry: A Manual for Investigative Journalists* (Paris, France: United Nations Educational, Scientific and Cultural Organization, Communication and Information Sector, Division for Freedom of Expression, Democracy and Peace, 2011), 8.

2 (definitions.net/definition/investigative-journalism), December 1, 2021.

3 David E. Kaplan, *Global Investigative Journalism: Strategies for Support: A Report to the Center for International Media Assistance*, 2nd ed. (Washington, D.C.: Center for International Media Assistance, 2013), 10.

Consequently, in order to do investigative journalism properly, reporters' employers have to provide environments in which journalists can work. This includes the time (days, weeks, months) the story or stories may require. In short, investigative journalism can be expensive to employers, no matter whether the reporters work for newspapers, magazines, radio stations, television stations, networks, or specific organizations that have been founded to do investigative journalism.

The Colonial Press

In the late 1600s and early 1700s, printers who owned coffeehouses or print shops read the latest newspapers from England, which were usually six months old, and heard the latest gossip from patrons and friends living in the colonies. In addition to selling coffee, these coffeehouses or print shops sold different items to the public. Eventually, these printers realized they may be able to earn additional income by printing a small newspaper of three or four pages.

The early newspapers typically contained very old news from Europe and some news—that is, information based primarily on gossip—about incidents that occurred in one or more colonies. Of course, the printers of these newspapers were not reporters or editors. They did not leave their businesses in order to interview individuals who knew what was happening in the colony. In fact, reporters did not start interviewing individuals until the 1800s.

Benjamin Harris

The earliest printer responsible for a newspaper (if one can call it a newspaper) in the colonies caused a stir. His name was Benjamin Harris. He was a printer in London who published religious tracts for the Anabaptists, a group that opposed Roman Catholicism and the Church of England. He also published a newspaper in which he "supported the Earl of Shaftesbury and the Whig parliament in their opposition to exclude the Duke of York (James II), Charles's Catholic brother, from succession to the throne."[4]

Primarily because of his eagerness to publish religious and political tracts as well as articles that were seen as controversial and seditious by those wielding power, Harris was arrested three times. Perhaps realizing that everything

4 William David Sloan and Julie Hedgepeth Williams, *The Early American Press, 1690–1782*, History of American Journalism Series (Westport, CT: Greenwood Press, 1994), 1:2.

he published would be scrutinized by the authorities, he set sail for America in 1686.

Arriving in Boston, Harris and his son opened a coffeehouse that, in addition to coffee, sold books. Soon, Harris became involved in printing almanacs and *The New-England Primer*, a collection of prayers and verses. Harris also realized that Boston's population was large enough to support a newspaper. On September 25, 1690, he published *Publick Occurrences, Both Forreign and Domestick*, the first newspaper in the American colonies.

Publick Occurrences, Both Forreign and Domestick differed from its broadside predecessors in the sense that it was a small, four-page publication that focused on American, not European, news. Indeed, several brief stories concerned the following: Christianized Indians planning a day of Thanksgiving, two children being abducted by Indians, the suicide of a widower, and the smallpox epidemic in Boston. A longer story concerned a confrontation by the militia of Massachusetts and the lack of cooperation by its Mohawk Indian allies against the French in Canada. The only European story concerned Louis XIV, the King of France, who had seduced his son's wife. According to the story, Louis XIV's son had revolted against him as a result.[5]

The authorities declared the paper a "pamphlet" and prohibited Harris from publishing another issue primarily because they did not approve of one or two stories. Although Harris did not publish another newspaper, he published other material. In fact, in 1692 he became the official printer of Massachusetts. A few years later he returned to London, where he published newspapers and other material.

Thereafter, colonial authorities required each printer who desired to print a newspaper to be approved by them. This demand had a cooling effect; it was almost fifteen years before another printer published a newspaper.

John Campbell

John Campbell, the postmaster of Boston, published *The Boston News-Letter* on April 24, 1704. To insure the newspaper was not stopped by the authorities, he did not include any article that could be considered controversial. He also printed "Published by Authority" at the top of the first page. Campbell continued publishing the newspaper for years, even after William Brooker replaced him as postmaster in 1719. Since Campbell's newspaper was no longer delivered through the mail, Brooker realized he could publish a rival

5 *Publick Occurrences, Both Forreign and Domestick*, September 25, 1690.

newspaper and distribute it through the mail. *The Boston Gazette* appeared on December 21, 1719.

James Franklin

Although James Franklin was born in Boston, he served as an apprentice to a printer in London. When he returned to Boston in 1717, he brought a press and some type with him. When William Brooker published *The Boston Gazette*, he hired James Franklin as the printer. Benjamin Franklin was James Franklin's younger brother and served as his apprentice. Unfortunately, when another postmaster took over the newspaper, he hired a different printer.

As a result, but against the advice of his friends, James founded *The New-England Courant*, a rival newspaper, on August 7, 1721. When a smallpox epidemic broke out in Boston, the clergy, including Increase and Cotton Mather, supported an inoculation program. Many Bostonians, including Dr. William Douglas, a friend of James Franklin, believed such a program would actually cause the disease to spread. *The New-England Courant* opposed the inoculation program. In fact, James criticized and even ridiculed the clergy, including the Mathers, which irritated the Mathers and the authorities. In 1722 James was arrested and served several weeks in jail.

When he was released, he continued to criticize the clergy and the authorities. In fact, he printed a so-called scandalous and libelous article that basically implied the colonial governor had been working with the pirates who sailed the Atlantic Ocean primarily because the governor had not apprehended them. The colonial governor was not amused. James was arrested in 1723 and again served time in jail. He was prohibited from publishing the paper. To appease the authorities, James pretended to turn the paper over to his younger brother, Benjamin. He actually advised Benjamin about the paper's content. Eventually, Benjamin left the paper and Boston primarily because of his brother's interference.

James kept the paper for a few more years. Then he moved to Rhode Island, where he died several years later.

Although *The New-England Courant* was not the second newspaper in the colonies, it was the second one to shock the authorities of New England. Primarily because of the several contributors to its pages, the newspaper was not only lively and entertaining, it was controversial. Fashioned after *The Spectator* of England, the paper contained satirical letters and topical essays, among other items of interest. Some of the content insulted the current postmaster of Boston and the printers of competing newspapers.[6]

Of course, most printers followed the rules established by the authorities, which were generally the governor and his subordinates. Only a few printers like Harris and Franklin and, later, John Peter Zenger tested the authorities. In essence, they rebelled primarily because of their convictions. They opposed those who attempted to rule or control others, especially printers who published newspapers. After all, the people who lived in the American colonies had left England and other countries to experience freedom in a new world.

John Peter Zenger

John Peter Zenger was born in the Rhenish Palatinate in 1697 and immigrated to the colonies with his family in 1710. Settling in New York, he became an apprentice in William Bradford's print shop. Marrying Mary White in 1719, he left New York and moved to Maryland. Within two years his wife died, leaving him with a son to support. Zenger returned to New York, where he married Anna Maulin in 1722.

Zenger worked briefly for Bradford before he opened a print shop in 1726. He published books, religious tracts, and a few government treatises, but he earned very little. He learned about the struggle between Lewis Morris and Stephen De Lancey; both were embroiled in politics. Later, he learned about the clash between Rip Van Dam, the president of the Provincial Council, and William Cosby, the new governor. Although Van Dam had been acting as governor until Cosby arrived, Cosby demanded that Van Dam return the salary he had been paid. Van Dam refused. Cosby decided to sue in the Provincial Supreme Court. Lewis Morris, the Chief Justice of the Supreme Court, refused to hear the case. Cosby removed Morris from the Supreme Court and appointed James De Lancey, Stephen De Lancey's son.

Those who opposed Cosby were members of the Popular Party. They realized that Bradford, the official printer for New York, would not necessarily print their views, so they approached Zenger, a struggling printer who needed their business.

Zenger published the first issue of *The New York Weekly Journal* on November 5, 1733. Zenger included "The Liberty of the Press," an article that caught the

6 Elizabeth Christine Cook, "Colonial Newspapers and Magazines, 1704–1775," *The Cambridge History of American Literature*, Vol. I, William Peterfield Trent, John Erskine, Stuart P. Sherman, and Carl Van Doren, eds. (New York: The Macmillan Company, 1954), 112.

attention of the authorities, in the second issue. Other articles considered radical for the time followed in other issues. Because of its editorial content the newspaper became popular. Cosby's administration was criticized and ridiculed. The war of words between the two sides continued in print. Cosby did not know who the writers were because they used pseudonyms, so he tried several times to have the printer charged with libel. Although Cosby was not successful, the Provincial Council brought action against Zenger, who was arrested in 1734. A trial by jury was scheduled, and, contrary to the authorities, Zenger was found innocent. Andrew Hamilton, Zenger's attorney, orchestrated a masterful defense, and Zenger's verdict triggered the dawn of liberty that revolutionized America.[7] In short, Hamilton claimed a printed statement was not libelous if it was based on fact.

In 1737 Zenger became the official printer for New York. A year later he became the official printer for New Jersey. He continued printing the paper until he died in 1746. His wife published the paper after his death.

* * *

As years passed other printers of newspapers exposed wrongdoings by colonial governors and their subordinates. However, as Mark Feldstein, who worked for major television networks such as CNN and who now holds the Richard Eaton Chair of Broadcasting Journalism at the University of Maryland, pointed out, "more often than not, these exposés were not necessarily based on fact but rumor."[8] Still, the early printers sowed the seeds of what would become known as investigative journalism.

By the mid-1750s newspapers contained more news items about public affairs and fewer items of literary satire, although several still included fictitious letters as well as a series of articles under a common title.

Before the American Revolutionary War, England exerted its power over the colonies by approving several acts and measures. In fact, the country seemed to tax the colonies for every military war it fought, no matter whether the war was fought on behalf of the colonies or not. As a result, newspapers included political essays that criticized Parliament. Eventually, newspapers

7 James Alexander, *A Brief Narrative of the Case and Trial of John Peter Zenger, Printer of the* New York Weekly Journal, Stanley Nider Katz, ed. (Cambridge, MA: Belknap Press of Harvard University Press, 1972; also Frank Luther Mott, *American Journalism: A History, 1690–1960*, 3rd ed. (New York: Macmillan, 1962), 31–38.

8 Mark Feldstein, "A Muckraking Model: Investigative Reporting Cycles in American History," *The International Journal of Press/Politics*, Vol. 11, No. 2 (April 1, 2006), 3.

carried essays that called for revolution. Several of these essays were written by individuals who would help found the United States of America.

The Revolutionary Press

During the American Revolutionary War printers of newspapers frequently lacked paper, type, and financial support, so most newspapers were not printed on a continuous basis. Even newspapers in the major cities such as Boston, New York, and Philadelphia were impacted.[9]

Printers of newspapers that were published attempted to cover the war as best they could. Of course, the coverage was generally biased or pro-colonies. After the war, newspapers included the "Declaration of Independence" as well as the various theories of government being discussed. Instead of focusing on news that had happened abroad, printers were concerned about the proceedings in Philadelphia.[10]

Most newspapers were small, contained no more than four pages, and were printed weekly. *The Pennsylvania Packet and Daily Advertiser*, which was printed three times a week, became the first daily in 1784.[11]

Several newspapers died during these years, but other newspapers were founded, particularly in the west. Unfortunately, circulation figures of newspapers were low. In fact, only a few in the larger cities reached a thousand readers. Printers suffered from few advertisements and late-paying subscribers, which, of course, caused printers not to earn much from each issue.

In addition to news about the new federal government, newspapers included stories about fires, murders, among other crimes, and other problems that occurred in the papers' vicinities. Several newspapers included various kinds of articles about trade and education, essays, and even poetry.[12]

The Political Party Press

Political parties, beginning with the Federalists, were responsible for numerous newspapers after the United States of America came into existence.

9 Frank W. Scott, "Newspapers, 1775–1860," *The Cambridge History of American Literature*, Vol. II, William Peterfield Trent, John Erskine, Stuart P. Sherman, and Carl Van Doren, eds. (New York: The Macmillan Company, 1954), 176.

10 Frank W. Scott, "Newspapers, 1775–1860," 177.

11 Frank W. Scott, "Newspapers, 1775–1860," 178.

12 Frank W. Scott, "Newspapers, 1775–1860," 179.

Indeed, George Washington had become the first president and had brought in Alexander Hamilton and other Federalists to serve in his administration. The Federalists, especially Hamilton, supported a relationship with England, a strong central government, and a national bank. Thomas Jefferson, another member of Washington's administration, favored a relationship with France, not England. He also opposed a strong central government primarily because he believed in states' rights. He opposed a national bank, too.

In order to inform the citizenry about the party and its goals, Hamilton, along with other Federalists, was responsible for the first political paper published in the country, which was John Fenno's *The Gazette of the United States*. The first issue was published in New York on April 15, 1789. Fenno supported Alexander Hamilton and the Federalists' almost monarchial control of the federal government in his newspaper.

To counter Hamilton and the Federalist Party's agenda, Thomas Jefferson and other Democratic Republicans persuaded Philip Freneau to publish *The National Gazette*. The first issue appeared on October 31, 1791. Freneau supported Thomas Jefferson's views, especially his belief that the federal government should be for and by the people.

Immediately, the war of words began, as these papers as well as others printed numerous scandalous and libelous personal attacks of politicians of the opposing party.[13] Truth was replaced with falsehoods filled with coarse language and name calling.

In addition, these newspapers often exposed corruption by politicians who were members of the opposing party. For instance, *The National Gazette* exposed corruption in the office of Alexander Hamilton. As a result, "several Hamilton aides at the Treasury Department were convicted for insider trading of government bonds."[14]

The National Gazette ceased publication on October 26, 1793, during the yellow fever epidemic in Philadelphia. As mentioned, the paper had supported Jefferson's view, but Jefferson had resigned as Secretary of State. Of course, there were other newspapers that supported Jefferson's view, including Benjamin Franklin Bache's *The Aurora and General Advertiser*.

13 Frank W. Scott, "Newspapers, 1775–1860," 181.

14 Mark Feldstein, "A Muckraking Model: Investigative Reporting Cycles in American History," 4.

Benjamin Franklin Bache

Bache, the grandson of Benjamin Franklin, accompanied his grandfather to Europe, where Benjamin saw to his formal education. Bache attended schools in France and Switzerland before he returned home several years later. He learned about printing from his grandfather and from working on a newspaper.

Bache was well-educated and well-read. He believed what his grandfather believed, too. Unlike his grandfather, however, he revealed his personal political biases through his newspaper. In fact, not only was he a strong supporter of Jefferson and the Democratic Republicans, he defended them by frequently attacking Hamilton and the Federalists. He even attacked George Washington, especially after the Jay Treaty, and John Adams. Although he was arrested for the scandalous articles he printed, he died from yellow fever in 1798, before his case went to trial.

* * *

The Gazette of the United States continued to support the cause of the Federalists. When Fenno died, his son, John Ward Fenno, became the editor. Later, the paper became *The United States Gazette*. Eventually, it was consolidated with *The Philadelphia North American*.

In 1798, primarily because the president and certain political leaders in Congress had grown tired of the vituperation of the party press, Congress passed the Alien and Sedition Acts in an effort to protect officials of the federal government from libelous statements made by individuals, no matter whether the statements were spoken or appeared in print.[15]

When Thomas Jefferson became president, his administration allowed the Alien and Sedition Acts to expire. However, about a dozen individuals had been convicted of libel before the act died. Most of these individuals were printers of Republican newspapers.[16]

Jefferson's old enemy Alexander Hamilton and the Federalists helped found *The New York Evening Post*, which appeared on November 1, 1801, and was edited by William Coleman. The purpose of the paper was to promote the Federalists and their cause and to destroy Jefferson. "If that purpose required the editor to vilify his party's opponents as liars and traitors, to attack the

15 Frank W. Scott, "Newspapers, 1775–1860," 181.

16 David Paul Nord, "Newspapers and American Nationhood, 1776–1826," *The Proceedings of the American Antiquarian Society*, Vol. 100, Part 2 (October, 1990), 401.

president as a moral degenerate with a slave harem, or to shoot a Republican dead in the street in a duel, so be it."[17]

James Thomson Callender became the editor of *The Richmond Recorder* in 1802. A friend of Jefferson's, Callender grew angry when Jefferson refused to offer a cabinet position to him, so he criticized Jefferson. In fact, he reported that Jefferson had an affair with one of his slaves. At the time, the story was based on rumors by anonymous sources.[18]

* * *

The number of newspapers increased, from under 200 in 1800 to more than 360 ten years later. Most of these newspapers were not dailies. In fact, there were fewer than thirty dailies in 1810.[19] Most of these papers were founded and supported by political parties. Although some newspapers ceased after a few years or when a political party was replaced by another, many endured for several decades, until certain conditions in journalism changed to the point that newspapers were no longer dependent on political parties for their existence.

About this time, editors, who were generally better educated, replaced printers of newspapers. Consequently, newspapers, particularly the content, improved over time. When the telegraph and railroad spread westward, newspapers no longer had to depend on those in Washington, D.C., as their primary source of political news. Editors came to realize that their readers were interested in local news, too.[20]

Yet, several newspapers supported by political parties still uncovered corruption in Washington, D.C., including the war of words between President Andrew Jackson and Nicholas Biddle, the president of the Bank of the United States at Philadelphia. Jackson was opposed to a national bank. In fact, he believed it was not supported by the constitution. He also believed it catered to the wealthy, not the poor, particularly when it came to loans. Of course, Jackson, a Democrat, realized the bank was supported by the Whig Party.

As a result of a resolution being passed by the directors of the bank in 1831, Biddle spent almost $30,000 between 1831 and 1834 in his efforts to persuade editors of newspapers to support the re-charter of the bank. Not only

17 David Paul Nord, "Newspapers and American Nationhood, 1776–1826," 392.

18 Christopher B. Daly, *Covering America: A Narrative History of a Nation's Journalism* (Amherst and Boston: University of Massachusetts Press, 2012), 53.

19 Frank W. Scott, "Newspapers, 1775–1860," 182.

20 Frank W. Scott, "Newspapers, 1775–1860," 183.

was this brought to the public's attention by the press, the bank was criticized for illegal practices, such as trading in public securities and speculating in real estate. The bank was even accused of establishing too many branches and putting the control of the bank in the hands of the exchange committee, of which Biddle was the head. Of course, there were other accusations that appeared in print.

When Jackson won reelection, he ordered all federal government deposits be removed from the bank. In addition, he refused to re-charter it. As a result, the bank became a state bank in Pennsylvania. However, articles about illegalities appeared in the press. Eventually, the bank collapsed in 1841. The stockholders lost their capital. Although Biddle had resigned in 1839, he was disgraced when he was charged for conspiring to cheat the stockholders. He escaped being sentenced to prison on a technicality.[21]

In essence, the political party press was interested mostly in political shenanigans, not other institutions such as businesses or companies. As a result, possible wrongdoing by businesses or companies or other institutions besides the federal government went largely unnoticed.[22]

Several editors at large newspapers realized that most of the political party papers were embarrassments because of the coarse language and name-calling used in much of the content. After all, they realized these papers existed for one reason: to criticize and ridicule politicians of the opposing party. Of course, they acknowledged these papers uncovered political corruption from time to time, but none had necessarily advanced journalism for the better.

Journalism changed as newspapers became less expensive to print because of the steam press. Readers were not charged as much per copy. As circulation figures increased, so did the number of advertisements, which helped defray the overall expenses. News values changed, too, along with reporting.[23]

21 William Graham Sumner, *Andrew Jackson* (Boston: Houghton Mifflin Company, 1910), 322–401.

22 Mark Feldstein, "A Muckraking Model: Investigative Reporting Cycles in American History," 4.

23 Frank W. Scott, "Newspapers, 1775–1860," 186.

The Penny Press

James Gordon Bennett, Sr.

Born in Scotland in 1795, James Gordon Bennett, Sr. immigrated to North America, arriving in Nova Scotia and ultimately moving to New York City. He had worked at several jobs in several cities before he found work as a correspondent for *The New York Enquirer*.

After a few attempts of starting a newspaper, Bennett finally started *The New York Herald* in 1835. Although he was not the first publisher to publish a newspaper that cost a penny, he was one of the earliest to thoroughly understand his readers' interests. Unlike the political party papers, which were partisan and dying almost every day, his newspaper was nonpartisan and filled with gossip and sensational reporting, including exposés about crime and Wall Street, among other subjects, and critical if not malicious stories about politicians. His reporters also covered foreign affairs, societal events, and sports. Bennett made sure his reporters included interviews whenever their stories needed them.[24] Of course, other penny papers, in order to compete, eventually included similar stories.

Bennett used the telegraph, carrier pigeons, and other means to make sure his newspaper had certain news before his competitors. It was not long before his paper enjoyed the largest circulation of any paper in New York City, if not the country.

* * *

In 1848 several newspapers in New York City founded the Associated Press for obtaining and sharing news. Later, other associations were founded for the same purpose.[25]

Steam ships replaced sailing vessels and consequently provided news from abroad in half the time. Several major newspapers sent correspondents to Europe, especially when wars broke out.

Publishers and editors of newspapers introduced specialized forms of journalism. For instance, they included news about agriculture, commerce, education, and religion. Other issues, including abolition, labor, prohibition, socialism, and temperance, among others, were covered as well. Of course, abolition had become a popular issue in the press primarily because it had

24 Frank W. Scott, "Newspapers, 1775–1860," 186.
25 Frank W. Scott, "Newspapers, 1775–1860," 187.

been discussed in newspapers that had been founded for that purpose. In fact, several editors had lost their lives because of their stand on the issue. Several newspapers were destroyed by fires.[26]

As mentioned, reporters improved their news stories when they included relevant interviews. They also improved stories that concerned businesses, financial firms, and markets. Letters from the editor or members of the staff became popular.[27] If the letter was based on what the writer had seen or heard, it was more popular.

Horace Greeley

Horace Greeley's *The New York Tribune* became one of the best-read newspapers because of its editorial positions toward the working man, women's rights, temperance reform, and capital punishment, among other causes and issues.[28]

Henry J. Raymond

Henry J. Raymond, who had worked for Greeley, started *The New York Times* on September 18, 1851. A conservative, Raymond's newspaper was not necessarily interested in controversial subjects.[29] (Over the years the paper changed hands. As a result, conservative editors and journalists were replaced with liberal editors and journalists. Consequently, the paper's content became liberal. In fact, several academicians who study the press believe it has become too liberal.)

The Press During and After the American Civil War

During the American Civil War, publishers of newspapers that provided the fullest accounts of battles saw their circulations increase. Generally, these were the larger papers. For instance, Bennett's newspaper had dozens and dozens of reporters covering the war. His readers learned about what happened during a particular battle before officials in the nation's capital did.

26 Frank W. Scott, "Newspapers, 1775–1860," 189.
27 Frank W. Scott, "Newspapers, 1775–1860," 190.
28 Frank W. Scott, "Newspapers, 1775–1860," 192.
29 Frank W. Scott, "Newspapers, 1775–1860," 194.

Charles A. Dana

After the war, Charles A. Dana of *The New York Sun* was responsible for using literary devices to weave stories about whatever happened. As Frank Scott put it, "This new style possessed simplicity and clearness; it abounded in details chosen for artistic effectiveness rather than for intrinsic news value."[30]

* * *

Eventually, newspaper publishers and editors returned to investigative journalism, particularly when Ulysses S. Grant, the former general and hero of the Civil War, became president. Grant had appointed individuals who became involved in all sorts of corruption. For instance, his vice president, Schuyler Colfax, had benefited from the Credit Mobilier of America affair, which involved a construction company that had charged the Union Pacific Railroad outlandish fees. Grant's secretary of war, W. W. Belknap, was forced to resign because he had taken bribes. Grant's secretary of the Treasury, W. W. Richardson, was implicated in an illegal scheme that had earned him money. Even Grant's private secretary, Orville Babcock, was accused of illegal activity and charged.[31]

As if these crimes were not enough to cause Americans to lose faith in their politicians and the federal government, other exposés revealed corruption, embezzlement, and graft by those who worked for major railroads, their lobbying organizations, and other businesses.

The New York Times, along with *Harper's Weekly*, exposed Boss William Tweed of New York City. As head of the Department of Public Works, Tweed had become the leader of Tammany Hall, the location of the Democrats. Tweed and his ring of sycophants traded small jobs for votes, which Tweed used to make certain specific politicians, judges, and district attorneys were elected. In short, he made sure certain legislation was passed by the New York legislature. Tweed and his sycophants employed all sorts of illegal means in order to fix deals and become wealthy. Eventually, Tweed was arrested and sent to prison.[32]

30 Frank W. Scott, "Newspapers Since 1860," *The Cambridge History of American Literature*, Vol. III, William Peterfield Trent, John Erskine, Stuart P. Sherman, and Carl Van Doren, eds. (New York: The Macmillan Company, 1954), 324.

31 Edd Applegate, *Political and Social Change in the United States: A Brief History, with the Articles of Confederation and Perpetual Union, the Declaration of Independence, the Constitution of the United States, and the Amendments to the Constitution* (Washington, D.C.: Academica Press, 2021), 33.

32 James L. Aucoin, *The Evolution of American Investigative Journalism* (Columbia: University of Missouri Press, 2006), 27–28.

Yellow Journalism

Joseph Pulitzer

Joseph Pulitzer had immigrated to the United States and had ultimately become the publisher of *The St. Louis Post-Dispatch.* He hired one or more reporters to investigate and write about various problems, including brothels, corrupt Democratic and Republican politicians, election fraud, gambling halls, monopolies, and questionable real estate deals.

Later, he moved to New York City, where he published *The New York World.* Facing competition, particularly when William Randolph Hearst, the publisher of *The San Francisco Examiner*, purchased *The New York Journal*, Pulitzer employed banner headlines, large illustrations, sensational exposés, and "The Yellow Kid," which was a cartoon of a boy dressed in yellow, to attract readers. Hearst soon hired Richard F. Outcault, the cartoonist of "The Yellow Kid," and several journalists from Pulitzer's *The New York World* in an effort to increase his newspaper's circulation. Pulitzer hired George B. Luks, another cartoonist, to draw a similar cartoon, and other journalists to replace those who had left. As the two publishers continued their furious competitiveness, especially for extraordinary investigative stories, the journalism appearing in their papers and eventually others became known as "yellow journalism."[33]

Fremont Older

On the West Coast, Fremont Older, perhaps the best editor overseeing any newspaper in California, was making waves, too.

Fremont was born on August 30, 1856, to Celia and Emory Older, near Appleton, Wisconsin. Fremont's father died from dysentery, which he had contracted in a military prison in Arkansas during the Civil War. Primarily because they were poor, Fremont and his family lived on his grandfather's farm.

When he was young, Fremont worked at different jobs. He attended a small religious school for a year, but that was the extent of his formal education. His mother remarried and moved to California, but Fremont remained in Wisconsin and became a printer's devil at *The Berlin Courant*, a small newspaper.

33 Frank W. Scott, "Newspapers Since 1860," 329–330.

Although he left the paper and briefly worked on a steamboat, he realized his experience as a printer's devil would help him find work at other newspapers.

Fremont moved to Hudson, Wisconsin, where his brother, Herbert, helped him get a job as a printer's devil at *The Hudson Democrat*. Later, Fremont was hired by the *St. Paul Pioneer Press* in Minnesota.

Fremont left St. Paul, briefly stopped in St. Louis, and then journeyed to southern Illinois, where his grandparents now lived. Soon, Fremont found a job with another newspaper.

In 1872 he moved to Chicago, where he briefly worked for *The Chicago Times*. Fremont left Chicago, visited relatives, and then worked at various small newspapers. After several months, he traveled to California.

Fremont visited his mother, and eventually worked at several small newspapers before he moved to San Francisco, where he worked for the *San Francisco Morning Call*. Fremont had read one or more novels by Mark Twain. When he learned that Twain had worked at the newspaper, he learned more about him. Soon, he followed Twain's footsteps and moved to Virginia City, Nevada, where he worked for the *Territorial Enterprise*.

In 1874 he returned to San Francisco and found a job at the *San Francisco Daily Mail*. After the *Daily Mail*, Fremont journeyed to Redwood City and worked as a reporter for the town's *Weekly Journal*. Fremont broadened his experience in journalism when he became the editor of the *Times-Gazette*.

He returned to San Francisco and worked for the *Daily Alta California* before he returned to the city's *Morning Call*. Fremont proved himself as a reporter in San Francisco. He married Cora Baggerly in 1893, and became the city editor at the *Morning Call* a year later.

In 1895 he was offered the position of managing editor of the *San Francisco Evening Bulletin*, which he accepted. Immediately, in an effort to increase the newspaper's circulation, Fremont developed stories that captured readers' attention. The *Evening Bulletin* became a more appealing product as a result. Although he experimented with different kinds of headlines in order to attract attention, his editorials caused readers to think about issues that pertained to San Francisco and California.

When young Theodore Durant murdered two women, Fremont realized that if the newspaper covered the murder, the accused, and his trial, the newspaper's circulation would increase, especially if the newspaper could beat its competition with story after story. When the reporter who covered the trial was able to get his story to the paper before his competitors, Fremont used "EXTRA" to announce the edition and news.

As a result of an increased circulation, the *Evening Bulletin*'s number of pages increased, and Fremont developed a Saturday edition that included news, editorials, poetry, and fiction. He also added a page devoted to sports and another devoted to articles for women. In short, Fremont's intuition about his readers enabled him to beat his competition.

Although Fremont did not write much for the newspaper, he provided ideas for stories and editorials to his staff. He was not afraid to use various sizes and fonts for headlines or stories. He experimented with layouts and artwork, too. In fact, he preferred artwork to photographs, which were used by some newspapers. Ultimately, the *Evening Bulletin* became one of the most attractive newspapers in the country. Of course, Fremont realized his readers, like readers everywhere, were interested in stories about murder and other acts of violence, so he did not disappoint them.

Primarily because he realized that San Francisco and California had politicians who had been corrupted by so-called "bosses," Fremont supported James Phelan, a candidate for mayor of San Francisco. Because of the newspaper's support, Phelan won the election. In fact, he served three terms. Unfortunately, Phelan was not interested in a fourth term. Eugene Schmitz, who was under the control of Abe Ruef, the so-called "boss" of San Francisco, won the election. Fremont, through the *Evening Bulletin*, tried to clean up the city by informing readers about the corruption. Eventually, Abe Ruef was arrested, convicted, and sentenced to prison. However, Fremont was not satisfied. He believed every person involved should have been arrested, convicted, and sentenced. Ironically, Fremont called for Ruef's freedom, which confused readers of the newspaper. To them, Fremont should have been satisfied that at least the so-called "boss" of the city had been sentenced to prison.

Fremont soon argued for prison reform as well as ending capital punishment. Of course, some readers respected the newspaper's position, but most did not.

In 1916, during World War I, a bomb exploded during a parade in San Francisco. Several individuals were killed and many were injured. Tom Mooney and a few others were arrested, convicted, and sentenced. Fremont believed Mooney and the others had been framed and were innocent. The newspaper argued for Mooney's freedom. Although there were questions about the district attorney, the primary witness, and the trial in general, Mooney was never released from prison.

Two years later the owner of the newspaper had had enough of Fremont's crusades, and Fremont found himself without a newspaper. However, William Randolph Hearst, who had been interested in hiring Older for some time, hired him as the editor of the *San Francisco Evening Call*. Fremont's journalistic skills caused the newspaper's circulation to increase within a year.

In addition to his job, Fremont enjoyed his life with Cora at their ranch. He read more and even wrote his first autobiography, *My Own Story*, which was published in 1919. He contributed a regular column to the newspaper, too.

When the *Evening Call* and the *San Francisco Evening Bulletin* merged in 1929, Fremont was named editor-in-chief. His second autobiography, *Growing Up*, was published in 1931.

On March 3, 1935, while driving home from a flower show in Sacramento, he died behind the wheel.[34]

* * *

In addition to the publishers and editors mentioned above, Joseph Medill, Adolph Ochs, E. W. Scripps and others had reporters investigate the various problems the country faced. In fact, these reporters exposed corruption that had infiltrated every level of government and big business. They examined numerous social problems, such as education, gambling, labor, prohibition, prostitution, and slums, among others. However, these exposés focused on local, not national, issues.

Nellie Bly (Elizabeth Cochrane)

Several of the investigative journalists who worked at the time became well known. For instance, Nellie Bly, who was actually Elizabeth Cochrane, was one of Pulitzer's more famous journalists.

Born in Pennsylvania, Bly was educated by her father until she was sent to a boarding school in Indiana. After a year she moved to Pittsburgh, where she contributed articles to *The Pittsburgh Dispatch*. Using the pseudonym "Nellie Bly," she investigated practically any business or municipal department she desired. She investigated factories, the theater, and art. She even contributed articles about her travels in the West.

Although she was offered a higher salary by the editor of the paper, she moved to New York City, where she found employment at *The New York*

34 Fremont Older, *My Own Story* (New York: The Macmillan Company, 1926; Fremont Older, *Growing Up* (San Francisco: San Francisco Call Bulletin, 1931).

World. In order to prove herself, Pulitzer allowed her to write whatever she was interested in. Soon, she committed herself to the insane asylum on Blackwell's Island. This experience was revealed in two of the most sensational and controversial stories of the period. According to Ishbell Ross, "She charged the nurses with goading their patients. She saw demented and gray-haired women dragged shrieking to hidden closets, then cries being stifled by force as they were hustled out of sight."[35] As a result of these stories, Blackwell Island was investigated by the authorities and subsequently improved.

Bly continued her investigations, exposing corrupt political lobbyists, the poor conditions of city prisons, the mistreatment of invalids, the poor conditions of old women's homes, and the mashers of Central Park.

She raced Jules Verne's fictitious Phileas Fogg of *Around the World in Eighty Days* in 1889. She wired interesting stories about her journey to the newspaper. When she returned, she had completed the trip in a little over seventy-two days.

Bly continued to write exposés for the paper. In 1895 she married a wealthy businessman who was considerably older. Eventually, she left the newspaper and journalism.[36]

Henry Demarest Lloyd

Another exceptional investigative reporter during this period was Henry Demarest Lloyd. After he was admitted to the New York bar, he became engaged in political reform. He campaigned against Tammany Hall in 1871. He campaigned for free trade and against the Republicans' nomination of Horace Greeley a year later. When he realized that newspapers could help him in his crusades, he accepted a position at *The Chicago Tribune*, where he wrote in-depth investigative articles about monopolies and their leaders, including John D. Rockefeller, William H. Vanderbilt, and Jay Gould.[37]

35 Ishbell Ross, *Ladies of the Press: The Story of Women in Journalism by an Insider* (New York: Harper and Brothers, 1936), 51.

36 For more information, see Brooke Kroeger, *Nellie Bly: Daredevil, Reporter, Feminist* (New York: Times Books, 1994); and Mignon Rittenhouse, *The Amazing Nellie Bly* (New York: E.P. Dutton, 1956).

37 For more information, see Chester McArthur Destler, *Henry Demarest Lloyd and the Empire of Reform* (Philadelphia: University of Pennsylvania Press, 1963); and Richard Digby-Junger, *The Journalist as Reformer: Henry Demarest Lloyd and Wealth Against Commonwealth* (Westport, CT: Greenwood Press, 1996).

Annie Laurie (Winifred Black)

Winifred Black or Annie Laurie invented stunts in order to obtain information and write sensational exposés. Educated in Illinois and Massachusetts, Black traveled to San Francisco and found employment as a reporter for *The San Francisco Examiner.*

Like many other reporters of this period, Black had to learn the techniques of journalism. The old impersonal style that had filled newspaper columns for years was changing. In fact, a more informal, lively, and hard-hitting style that attracted readers and mirrored the time was becoming more popular among publishers, particularly Hearst, and editors.

Black's early stories were stilted and filled with too many adjectives. However, she persevered until she knew how to compose personal, vivid prose. She also learned how to investigate and obtain information of interest.

For one of her exposés she fainted on a San Francisco street so she would be brought to the receiving hospital. She observed that she and other patients were neglected. Her story criticized the care of patients and as a result the city was forced to dismiss several hospital employees in order to improve patient care.

Her articles about "Little Jim," a crippled boy born to a prostitute in San Francisco's prison hospital, helped launch a campaign that ultimately provided a ward for incurables at the city's Children's Hospital.

Black continued to write journalism for Hearst. In addition to exposés, she interviewed prominent individuals. She covered the suffragettes in England. She investigated the juvenile court system in Chicago and the Charity Organization Society in New York City. She covered the devastating hurricane in Galveston, Texas, the earthquake in San Francisco, and World War I. She remained a reporter until her death in 1935.[38]

Jacob Riis

Another investigative journalist during this period was Jacob Riis, who immigrated to the United States with the intention of working as a carpenter. However,

38 For more information, see Katherine H. Adams and Michael L. Keene, *Winifred Black/Annie Laurie and the Making of Modern Nonfiction* (Jefferson, N.C.: McFarland & Company, Inc., 2015); Barbara Belford, *Brilliant Bylines: A Biographical Anthology of Notable Newspaperwomen in America* (New York: Columbia University Press, 1986); and Faye B. Zuckerman, "Winifred Black," *Dictionary of Literary Biography: American Newspaper Journalists, 1901–1925, Vol. 25*, edited by Perry J. Ashley (Detroit: Gale, 1984).

construction jobs were scarce. Finally, after a few years, he landed a job at one of the news associations in New York City.

In 1877 he became a police reporter for *The New York Tribune*. Riis frequented the police headquarters for the East Side slum district, where he met poor immigrants who had been arrested by the police. He visited the filthy tenements in which the immigrants lived. As he learned the reasons for the medieval conditions, he realized the public needed to be informed. Through numerous investigations and interviews, he learned that the property of the lower East Side was owned by those who cared little about the conditions in which immigrants lived. In fact, landlords neglected the property. The politicians cared little about the criminals, pimps, prostitutes, beggars, drunks, tramps, and homeless children who wandered the streets.

Riis wrote numerous stories that depicted the inhumane conditions. He exposed the cruelty involved and the pain of these victims. He advocated for improvements. Finally, in 1884 his efforts caused the Tenement House Commission to be formed. The commission investigated his claims and acted.

Riis's popularity grew. In 1888 *How the Other Half Lives*, his monumental book, was published.

Riis died in 1914.[39]

* * *

Exposés were growing in popularity among publishers and editors of newspapers. However, magazine publishers and editors realized, too, the significance in-depth investigative reporting played. Soon, this investigative journalism became known as "muckraking journalism."

Muckraking Journalism

President Theodore Roosevelt applied "muckrake" to the journalism appearing in print when he delivered a speech in the spring of 1906 in Washington, D.C. Roosevelt compared certain crusading journalists to a character in John Bunyan's *Pilgrim's Progress*:

39 For more information, see James B. Lane, *Jacob A. Riis and the American City* (Port Washington, NY: Kennikat Press, 1974); Edith Patterson Meyer, *"Not Charity, But Justice": The Story of Jacob A. Riis* (New York: Vanguard Press, 1974); and Louise Ware, *Jacob A. Riis: Police Reporter, Reformer, Useful Citizen* (New York: Appleton-Century Co., 1938).

> There is filth on the floor, and it must be scraped up with the muckrake, and there are times and places where this service is the most needed of all the services that can be performed. But the man who never does anything else, who never thinks or speaks or writes save of his feats with the muckrake, speedily becomes, not a help to society, not an incitement to good, but one of the most potent forces of evil.[40]

Roosevelt criticized every crusading journalist who wrote exposés during this period. These journalists "had exposed the massive injustices and corruptions of an American society that, in its greed, had cast overboard all concepts of honor and most of the principles of true democratic government."[41]

Roosevelt thought his comments would curtail such journalism, but journalists continued writing exposé articles and books for years after his speech.

In addition to Roosevelt, there were other individuals who criticized muckraking journalism, including several journalists. For instance, H. L. Mencken, a journalist who had written a few exposés earlier in his career but who had gained prominence primarily because of his numerous editorials for *The Baltimore Sun* and his criticism for *The Smart Set*, believed publishers and editors were interested in this form of journalism because it captured readers' attention and increased profits.[42]

Just what is muckraking journalism? According to Harry H. Stein and John M. Harrison, "Muckraking is associated with four major press traditions in America. It bears closest resemblance to investigative journalism; less, to advocacy journalism. It has a distant relation to sensationalistic and to yellow journalism.... "[43]

In essence, muckraking journalism occurs when a journalist or writer suspects that there may be a problem in the business sector, political sector, or social sector, and then investigates the problem to determine if it actually exists. Finally, the journalist or writer reports about the problem.

Although muckraking articles had appeared in several newspapers, most appeared in magazines in the late 1800s and early 1900s. In fact, many of these articles appeared in the *American Magazine*, the *Arena*, *Collier's*, *Cosmopolitan*, the *Era*, *Everybody's Magazine*, *Hampton's Magazine*, *Human*

40 Fred J. Cook, *The Muckrakers: Crusading Journalists Who Changed America* (Garden City, N.J.: Doubleday and Company, 1972), 10.

41 Fred J. Cook, *The Muckrakers*, 8.

42 James L. Aucoin, *The Evolution of American Investigative Journalism*, 36.

43 John M. Harrison and Harry H. Stein, "Muckraking Journalism in Twentieth-Century America," *Muckraking: Past, Present and Future*, John M. Harrison and Harry H. Stein (University Park: Pennsylvania State University Press, 1973), 14.

Life, *The Independent*, *McClure's Magazine*, *Metropolitan Magazine*, *The Outlook*, *Pearson's Magazine*, *Success Magazine*, *Twentieth Century Magazine*, *The World To-Day*, and *World's Work*, among others. According to Donald A. Ritchie, the historian emeritus of the United States Senate and the author of several nonfiction books, "Muckraking magazines took their cues from crime reporting and created images of widespread corruption in local and national government. Their exposés were theatrical, and they sold, vastly expanding magazine circulations."[44]

The most productive muckraking journalists who wrote for magazines were Charles Edward Russell, Thomas W. Lawson, Ray Stannard Baker, Ida Tarbell, Burton J. Hendrick, Lincoln Steffens, C. P. Connally, Samuel Hopkins Adams, and Will Irwin, among others. These muckrakers and others investigated big business, child labor, crime, education, the federal government, labor problems, local government, meat-packing plants, political corruption, the press, prohibition, prostitution, religion, slums, state government, the stock market, and utilities, among other topics.

In addition to writing exposés for magazines, several of these journalists and others wrote insightful books in which the above topics and others were investigated and exposed.

Charles Edward Russell

For instance, Charles Edward Russell worked as a reporter and editor at several newspapers, including *The Detroit Tribune*, *The New York Herald*, *The New York World*, *The New York American*, and *The Chicago American*, among others.

In 1905 the editor of *Everybody's Magazine* asked him to write several articles about the meatpacking industry. The series was titled "The Greatest Trust in the World," and Russell explained how the industry had become more powerful than the federal government.

Russell wrote other muckraking articles about child labor, corruption in the railroad industry, election fraud, and individuals who had made fortunes under questionable circumstances for the same publication. He contributed similar exposés to *Hampton's Magazine*.

Russell wrote several muckraking books based on material he had gathered for several articles as well as a few biographies.[45]

44 Donald A. Ritchie, "The Power of the Press," *Reviews in American History*, Vol. 15, No. 2 (June, 1987), 206.

45 For more information, see Robert Miraldi, *The Pen Is Mightier: The Muckraking Life of Charles Edward Russell* (New York: Palgrave Macmillan, 2003); and Charles Edward

Thomas W. Lawson

Thomas W. Lawson left school when he was twelve and went to work in a brokerage firm in Boston. By the time he was twenty, he was worth several hundred thousand dollars. Lawson became a broker and assisted several prominent individuals in their business negotiations. By 1900 he was worth several million dollars.

Primarily because he knew about several businesses, including the Standard Oil Company, and how these companies had manipulated the system for profits, the owners of *Everybody's Magazine* persuaded him to write several articles for the magazine. Lawson's series was titled "Frenzied Finance," in which he explained how the system operated and claimed the system, itself, was at fault, not the men who had taken advantage of it. As a result of his series, the magazine's circulation quadrupled to almost a million copies every month in 1905.[46] The series also influenced the governor of New York to appoint a committee to investigate. Officials of several companies were either indicted or forced to resign. The series also was published as a book.

In 1912 Lawson wrote another series titled "The Remedy" for the magazine. In this series, Lawson presented the problems of Wall Street and suggested several solutions. The series was not as popular as the earlier series, but it caught the attention of several senators. Like the previous series, the articles were published as a book later the same year.[47]

Ray Stannard Baker

Ray Stannard Baker became one of the most prolific muckraking journalists in the country. Well-educated, he found employment as a reporter for *The Chicago News-Record*. He traveled to Canton, Ohio, and interviewed Jacob Coxey, who was leading an army of the downtrodden to Washington, D. C. Coxey and the poor people he was leading were hoping the federal government would help them. Baker interviewed other members of the army and grew to understand their cause.

Russell, *Bare Hands and Stone Walls: Some Recollections of a Sideline Reformer* (New York: Charles Scribner's Sons, 1933).

46 For more information, see Edd Applegate, *Muckrakers: A Biographical Dictionary of Writers and Editors* (Lanham, MD: The Scarecrow Press, Inc., 2008), 91–95.

47 For more information, see Louis Filler, *Crusaders for American Liberalism* (New York: Harcourt, Brace & Co., 1939).

Whenever the paper needed a reporter to cover a particular labor disturbance, the editor thought of Baker. For instance, when the Pullman strike occurred, he covered it. In fact, he was indignant about what he observed. Although the company had constructed homes for employees, many of the occupants were starving. Ultimately, a relief bureau was established.

Baker's reputation spread. By 1898 he was working for *McClure's Magazine*, which became one of the leading muckraking magazines. Baker wrote about labor, specifically about employee abuse and labor unions.

In 1905 he exposed railroad corruption in a series of articles. As a result of this series and other articles, railroads were finally regulated when the Hepburn Act was passed the same year.

Baker, along with several other muckraking journalists, purchased what became the *American Magazine*, for which he wrote several series, including "Following the Color Line." This series concerned the racial problem in the country.

In 1915 Baker resigned from the magazine and devoted most of his time to Woodrow Wilson's writings. Baker then wrote his autobiography, which was published in two volumes, in the 1940s.[48]

Ida Tarbell

Ida Tarbell graduated from Allegheny College and then worked at the *Chautauquan* for several years. In 1892 S. S. McClure of *McClure's Magazine* persuaded her to write several biographies of famous individuals. Later, she investigated the Standard Oil Company and wrote nineteen articles for the magazine. Tarbell revealed that the company was well managed. Although it operated smoothly, the company had been built with bribery, fraud, and even violence. As a result of the articles, Tarbell became well known. However, she was not objective in her articles primarily because her father had been put out of business by the company. In fact, she was not necessarily respected by businessmen and politicians who had a high regard for the company.

Along with several other muckraking journalists, she purchased what became the *American Magazine*, for which she wrote articles about the tariff

48 For more information, see Ray Stannard Baker, *Native American: The Book of My Youth* (New York: Charles Scribner's Sons, 1941); Robert C. Bannister, *Ray Stannard Baker; the Mind and Thought of a Progressive* (New Haven, CT: Yale University Press, 1966); and John E. Semonche, *Ray Stannard Baker; a Quest for Democracy in Modern America, 1870–1918* (Chapel Hill: University of North Carolina Press, 1969).

and women. She was not sympathetic to the suffrage movement, however. Although she wrote articles about other topics, including Henry Ford's assembly line, she resigned from the magazine in 1915.[49]

Burton J. Hendrick

Burton J. Hendrick graduated from Yale in 1895, and worked as a reporter and an editor at a small newspaper. Later, he found employment as a reporter for *The New York Evening Post*. He wrote detailed accounts for the newspaper and contributed in-depth investigative articles to magazines. S. S. McClure of *McClure's Magazine* offered him a position and he accepted. Hendrick exposed the good and bad of the insurance business in "The Story of Insurance." In fact, he discussed the men who had made the insurance profession one of the best in the world. Then he focused on the corrupt men who had degraded it.

Hendrick stayed at the magazine until 1913. However, most of the articles he wrote paled in comparison to the series about insurance.

He wrote several books, including biographies, after he left *McClure's* and, later, *World's Work*.[50]

Lincoln Steffens

Lincoln Steffens, another muckraking journalist, worked as a reporter for *The New York Evening Post* and as a city editor at *The New York Commercial Advertiser* before he joined *McClure's Magazine*. He traveled to various cities and wrote several muckraking articles about corrupt politicians, police forces, and other municipal departments. In 1904 a collection of his city articles was published under the title, *The Shame of the Cities*.

Steffens turned his attention to state governments and wrote several articles about how certain politicians were fighting corruption within their states.

Although he, along with several other muckraking journalists, purchased what would become the *American Magazine*, he resigned soon after and worked as an editor at *Everybody's Magazine*.

49 For more information, see Kathleen Brady, *Ida Tarbell: Portrait of a Muckraker* (New York: Seaview/Putnam's, 1984); Ida M. Tarbell, *All in the Day's Work* (New York: Macmillan Co., 1939); and Mary E. Tomkins, *Ida M. Tarbell* (New York: Twayne Publishers, 1974).

50 For more information, see David Mark Chalmers, *The Social and Political Ideas of the Muckrakers* (New York: Citadel Press, 1964); Lewis Filler, *The Muckrakers* (University Park: Pennsylvania State University Press, 1968); and Harold S. Wilson, *McClure's Magazine and the Muckrakers* (Princeton, NJ: Princeton University Press, 1970).

Steffens traveled in the United States and reported about what he found. Then he traveled to Europe, where he gathered information about various cities. He traveled to Mexico and then to Europe again. He studied the revolution in Russia. He covered the armistice negotiations. He interviewed Vladimir Lenin. After several years, he returned to the states and made his home in California, where he wrote his autobiography.[51]

C. P. Connally

C. P. Connally was born in 1863 in the state of New York. He studied law and became the assistant district attorney in Butte, Montana. Later, he became the prosecuting attorney.

He moved to Missoula, Montana, and practiced law. He wrote the muckraking series "The Story of Montana," which concerned the controversial differences between the mining companies and the miners in the state, for *McClure's Magazine*. He also presented the early history of the state as well as the rise of the copper kings who controlled the state's corrupt government.

Connally investigated other topics for the magazine. For instance, he examined William Howard Taft's administration's western land policy in the article "Can This Be White-Washed Also?"

His series "Big Business and the Bench," which described the unethical relationship between business and the judiciary, was published in *Everybody's Magazine* several years later, after he moved to New Jersey.

Connally investigated public figures in Washington, D.C., and their connections to big business and wrote "Undesirable Senators." He also wrote articles about famous trials for different magazines.

Although he was primarily a lawyer, his articles performed a public service.[52]

Samuel Hopkins Adams

Samuel Hopkins Adams, another muckraking journalist, graduated from Hamilton College in 1891. He worked for *The New York Sun* before he was

51 For more information, see Russell M. Horton, *Lincoln Steffens* (New York: Twayne Publishers, 1974); Justin Kaplin, *Lincoln Steffens; a Biography* (New York: Simon & Schuster, 1974); and Lincoln Steffens, *The Autobiography of Lincoln Steffens* (New York: Harcourt, Brace & Co., 1931).

52 For more information, see John Daniel Main, *Four Muckrakers: Lawson, Hendrick, Connolly, and French; a Critical Analysis*, Thesis (Pittsburg: Kansas State College of Pittsburg, 1963).

hired by S. S. McClure in 1900. However, he left *McClure's Magazine* five years later to write articles and books.

His series about the patent medicine industry was published in *Collier's* in 1905. Titled "The Great American Fraud," the series exposed the addictive "tonics" that were being sold in various stores in the country. The series played an important role in the passage of the Pure Food and Drug Act of 1907.

In 1915 and 1916, he contributed a series about deceptive advertising to *The New York Tribune*.

Adams spent the rest of his life writing short stories, novels, biographies, and books for children.[53]

Marion Hamilton Carter

Better known as a writer of short stories and a few novels, Marion Hamilton Carter wrote several muckraking articles for *McClure's Magazine* in the early 1900s. Carter had attended several colleges, including Cornell University, from which she received her bachelor's degree in 1898. She had enrolled in graduate courses, intending to earn a graduate degree, but she never finished the requirements. She taught elementary education for several years. Her experiences in the classroom provided enough information for several articles.

In 1899, for instance, she wrote "The Kindergarten Child—After the Kindergarten," which was published in the March issue of *The Atlantic Monthly*. In essence, Carter criticized kindergarten education, which caused several prominent educators to question her criticism. In 1904 her article "The Parent," was published in the November issue of *McClure's Magazine*. Carter categorized different types of parents who had children in elementary schools and proceeded to criticize each one.

Two years later Carter covered the Josephine Terranova trial. Terranova had murdered her aunt and uncle primarily because they had abused her as a child. Carter concentrated on Terranova's psychological state at the time in her articles.

In 1908 she returned to criticizing kindergarten education in "The Juvenile Joy School." The article, which appeared in the October issue of *The Housekeeper*, was part of the publication's "The Truth about Public Schools" series.

53 For more information, see Samuel P. Kennedy, *Samuel Hopkins Adams and the Business of Writing* (Syracuse, NY: Syracuse University Press, 1999).

In 1909 Carter wrote "The Conservation of the Defective Child," which was published in the June issue of *McClure's Magazine*. The article concerned several physical and mental problems that effected children and their ability to learn. The same year she journeyed to the Carolinas, where two epidemics had killed thousands of people over a few years. "The Vampire of the South" was published in the October 1909 issue of *McClure's Magazine*. Carter presented the history of hookworm, which had caused one of the epidemics, as well as the current medical research about it. "Pellagra: The Medical Mystery of To-day" appeared in the November 1909 issue of the same magazine. Pellagra had caused the other epidemic, particularly among the poor, in 1906. Similar to the previous article, Carter discussed the history of pellagra and the current medical research about it.

Carter wrote other articles, too, including several that were published in scholarly publications. She was also active in the women's suffrage movement.

She died in 1937.[54]

A few of the muckraking journalists mentioned above included their socialistic leanings in their writing. Others presented just the facts without any editorializing. Several ridiculed their subjects by offering opinions as facts. Others were selective in their facts in order to present only one side.[55]

Of course, there were other muckraking journalists. However, like the above, they were forced, for the most part, to write other kinds of journalism when muckraking journalism declined in popularity during World War I. The reasons for the decline included one or more of the following: readers' interests had changed; magazines had been purchased by more conservative companies; editors had been forced to publish other forms of journalism; publishers had seen their advertising dollars decrease; and/or the muckraking journalists had grown tired of spending weeks, months, or years investigating a subject.

54 Mary Maillad, "Biographical Sketch of Marion Hamilton Carter, 1865–1937," *Part III: Mainstream Suffragists—National American Woman Suffrage Association, Online Biographical Dictionary of the Woman Suffrage Movement in the United States*, Thomas Dublin and Kathryn Kish Sklar, eds. (documents.alexanderstreet.com/d/1011002167), March 5, 2022.

55 Tim V. Klein, "Single Out the Rascals for Distinction from Their Fellows: Realist, Prosecutorial, Yellow, and Radical Muckraking in the Progressive Era," *Media History Monographs*, Vol. 21, No. 1 (2019), 1.

Of course, several magazines that had published muckraking journalism closed because of mismanagement or a lack of advertisers.[56] In other words, the number of readers of these magazines had decreased probably because the readers desired to learn about the war in Europe primarily because they were afraid that President Woodrow Wilson, a progressive Democrat, would break his promise, which was to keep the United States out of the war. Or they had grown tired of the Progressive Movement.

At the same time, publishers and editors had grown interested in journalism that was more objective. In short, they thought journalists should leave their opinions and beliefs out of their stories.[57] Because of this change on the part of publishers and editors, major problems that reared their ugly heads went largely unreported.

* * *

Investigative journalism did not die, however. After World War I, publishers and editors of major metropolitan newspapers and news magazines assigned occasional investigative exposés to one or more reporters.[58] Most of this journalism focused on subjects relevant to the market in which the publications served. Fewer articles focused on national problems. Instead of investigative articles about the federal government or large businesses, publishers and editors favored articles about their local governments and businesses.[59]

Before World War I, readers noticed fewer muckraking articles in mass-circulated magazines. Yet, several of the muckraking articles or series of articles that had appeared in these magazines had been indirectly responsible for several major pieces of legislation that helped or improved conditions in the country.

Investigative Journalism after the Muckraking Period

Even though reporters still researched and wrote investigative journalism, none uncovered the scandals that occurred during President Warren G.

56 Rosemary Armao, "The History of Investigative Reporting," *The Big Chill: Investigative Reporting in the Current Media Environment*, Marilyn S. Greenwald and Joseph Bernt, eds. (Ames, IA: Iowa State University Press, 2000), 39.

57 James L. Aucoin, *The Evolution of American Investigative Journalism*, 37.

58 Rosemary Armao, "The History of Investigative Reporting," 39.

59 James L. Aucoin, *The Evolution of American Investigative Journalism*, 37–38; also Rosemary Armao, "The History of Investigative Reporting," 39.

Harding's administration. For instance, the director of the Veterans Bureau had sold government supplies at low prices and the secretary of the interior had sold leases of government land to oil companies. The latter had received several hundred thousand dollars in return. This scandal became known as Teapot Dome, which was the name that had been given to the oil reserve in Wyoming. Ultimately, Albert D. Fall, the secretary of the interior, was charged for accepting bribes and sentenced to prison.[60] The scandals were investigated by the U. S. Senate, however, not the press. In fact, the press merely followed the Senate's investigation.

After the muckraking period, the press was apprehensive, if not negligent, in its responsibilities to uncover corruption. In fact, seldom did it have the courage or inclination to have reporters spending days, weeks, or months investigating a major problem or problems in Washington and elsewhere. Yet, after World War I, primarily in the 1920s, numerous problems such as labor disputes and racketeering existed. In fact, the latter was responsible for major crimes, including bribery, murder, and prostitution. It was responsible for numerous speakeasies, too.

If an incident like one of the above happened, a reporter typically gathered the facts from the police and wrote a story about the incident. The reporter seldom spent days, weeks, or months investigating the incident. On the other hand, there were former journalists like Louis Adamic who wrote articles and book-length exposés about such incidents. For example, Adamic wrote *Dynamite: The Story of Class Violence in America*, which concerned the senseless violence caused by labor.[61]

When the 1930s began, it seemed the press grew more accepting of presidential economic blunders that basically caused the Great Depression. When Franklin D. Roosevelt, a Democrat, became president, it was as if reporters felt sorry for him because of his health or had too much respect for him to seriously investigate him. After all, he was well-educated and had experience working for the government. Unfortunately, newspaper reporters let the public down by not investigating him or his administration. For instance, they did not mention his poor health or his interest in other women besides his wife. Nor did they report about his administration's numerous mistakes concerning the economy. As a result, too many people lost their jobs. On the other hand, Roosevelt provided hope and his administration instituted numerous

60 Edd Applegate, *Political and Social Change in the United States*, 54.

61 Edd Applegate, *Muckrakers*, 1.

programs that offered employment. And two or three of the programs, such as the Tennessee Valley Authority, actually benefited the country. But only one or two of the programs lowered unemployment for a long period of time. In fact, only when the United States entered World War II did the economy really improve.[62]

Of course, the press was suffering, too, economically speaking. Before 1920 the number of newspapers started to decline. Some cities had too many newspapers for the reading public. In other words, the reading public in these cities could not support every newspaper printed. Consequently, one or more papers in these cities were purchased and merged into another paper or, worse, closed. Several publishers had purchased too many newspapers and were in debt. As their readerships declined, their subscriptions and advertising revenues decreased as well. To make matters worse, radio, a new medium, was growing more popular every day.

During the Great Depression, in order to save money, readers of newspapers and magazines stopped their subscriptions. This action added to the problems these media were experiencing.

The Great Depression and the problems associated with it, particularly at the local level, were covered by the press. By the mid-1930s readers were growing interested in the actions of political leaders, specifically Adolf Hitler, in Europe. Although many Americans were suffering economically, they were afraid that another Democratic President would break his promise by involving the United States in another war. Even though President Roosevelt assured them he would not, when the Japanese bombed Pearl Harbor, he asked members of Congress for a declaration of war.

For the next several years, newspaper and magazine editors and publishers had correspondents covering the war in Europe and, later, in Asia. The press in the United States covered the war well, even though certain reporters were overly critical of one or more generals of the United States. In fact, these reporters seemed to favor the British more than they favored the Americans in what and how they wrote. Of course, they may have been basing their stories on so-called official information from the administration in Washington or from the military, not necessarily from what they had observed. Or their stories had been edited by a member of the administration or the military or an editor at the newspaper.

62 Edd Applegate, *Political and Social Change in the United States*, 59–69.

George Seldes

While correspondents covered the war, George Seldes gathered information for his four-page weekly newspaper, *In Fact*, which he had founded in 1940. Seldes had worked for several newspapers before World War I and had written several books before World War II. For his small newspaper he wrote controversial stories that major newspapers overlooked or would not print, such as exposing the link between members of the National Association of Manufacturers (NAM) and Nazi Germany and Fascist Italy.[63]

* * *

After World War II, the press, like other institutions in the United States, grew somewhat complacent as a result of the war being over. It was a time to celebrate. Besides, the economy had rebounded because of the war.

By the time former General Dwight David Eisenhower, who had been in charge of the military efforts in Europe, became president, many newspapers and magazines were owned by chains. Publishers of these publications had become wealthy over the years. Consequently, they tended to promote the status quo and free enterprise. These publishers were not necessarily interested in investigative journalism, unless something major happened in a city where one of their newspapers was located.

Although the country was improving economically, during the 1950s the federal government grew paranoid toward the Soviet Union and its efforts to spread communism. Senator Joseph McCarthy of Wisconsin, for instance, made sure of that by speaking often to the press, claiming he had lists of federal employees who were known communists or sympathizers to those who were. Of course, initially, publishers, editors, and reporters believed the senator. In fact, publishers of major metropolitan newspapers tended to cooperate with the federal government in its fight against communism. Although fascism had been defeated in World War II, communism had not. Eventually, Murrey Marder of *The Washington Post*, who had covered the Alger Hiss trial, investigated Senator Joseph McCarthy. In 1953 Marder claimed Senator McCarthy's accusations about espionage agents working at Fort Monmouth, New Jersey, were false. In 1954 Edward R. Murrow, the host of the program "See It Now" on CBS, one of the three major television networks at the time, interviewed

63 For more information, see George Seldes, *Witness to a Century: Encounters With the Noted, the Notorious, and the Three SOBs* (New York: Ballantine Books, 1987); and Derek Shearer, "George Seldes: Muckraker Emeritus," *Ramparts*, 12, No. 2 (August–September, 1973).

Senator McCarthy and revealed the senator could not necessarily prove what he claimed. Marder's stories, not to mention Murrow's interview, led to the Army-McCarthy hearings, which embarrassed the senator. Later, McCarthy was investigated and censured by the United States Senate. Later, Murrow investigated the plight of migrants who worked on farms.[64]

I. F. Stone

During this period, after having worked for several newspapers and magazines, I. F. Stone founded *I. F. Stone's Weekly*, a small newspaper. His publication contained accurate exposés with subtle humor. Stone uncovered facts that other journalists had overlooked. He included quotations from officials in Washington that contradicted other sources. Stone revealed numerous inconsistencies as well as lies in his stories.[65] Another small newspaper of this period was *The Village Voice*, which included a column by Norman Mailer, one of the newspaper's founders, as well as investigative stories by different writers.

Drew Pearson

Before President Eisenhower left office, one of his assistants, Sherman Adams, was investigated by Jack Anderson, who worked for Drew Pearson. Pearson had the column "The Washington Merry-Go-Round," in which he disclosed that Adams had helped Bernard Goldfine, a businessman, through the federal maze in Washington. In return, Goldfine had given gifts to Adams. The report by Pearson caused other journalists to question the assistant's actions. As a result, Adams resigned from his position. Of course, Pearson, before Anderson had joined his staff, had investigated other prominent individuals in Washington, including Secretary of War Patrick J. Hurley.

Anderson collaborated with Pearson on the book *U.S.A.: Second-Class Power?*, which was published in 1958. The authors criticized the Eisenhower administration, specifically its policies that stymied scientific progress.

In the 1960s Pearson exposed Attorney General Robert F. Kennedy's authorization to spy on Dr. Martin Luther King, Jr., who headed peaceful

64 David L. Protess, Fay Lomax Cook, Jack C. Doppelt, James S. Ettema, Margaret T. Gordon, Donna R. Leff, and Peter Miller, *The Journalism of Outrage: Investigative Reporting and Agenda Building in America* (New York: The Guilford Press, 1991), 46.

65 For more information, see Robert C. Cottrell, *Izzy: A Biography of I. F. Stone* (New Brunswick, NJ: Rutgers University Press, 1992); and Andrew Patner, *I. F. Stone: A Portrait* (New York: Pantheon Books, 1988).

demonstrations for civil rights for African Americans. He also exposed Thomas J. Dodd, who had diverted monies from dinners and contributions to his campaigns to his personal account. Dodd eventually was censured by the U. S. Senate.[66]

* * *

Only a few journalists were engaged in serious investigative reporting in the 1950s and early 1960s. Besides Drew Pearson and Jack Anderson, there was Fred J. Cook, who wrote exposés about corruption in government and big business. He also wrote about prominent individuals, including criminals and politicians.[67] Tad Szulc, who worked for *The New York Times*, covered several coups in South America. For instance, he examined the overthrow of Juan Peron in Argentina. He wrote an in-depth report about President John F. Kennedy's Bay of Pigs invasion, which was a disaster. In fact, he wrote numerous exposés about political issues in Washington.[68]

In the 1960s the federal government used the press to disseminate information about the Vietnam War. Primarily because the press failed to investigate the information, several so-called factual statements in the information were false. For instance, the body count of the enemy was inflated periodically. Yet, this information appeared in newspapers and broadcast on television. As if this was not grave enough, reporters found themselves being used by those wielding power. President Lyndon B. Johnson successfully manipulated reporters for several years. In fact, they accepted what he told them or what his administration provided without questioning it. Only when information about the Vietnam War conflicted with reports by journalists covering the war did President Johnson and his administration have problems. Of course, previous presidents had lied to the American people. President Dwight David Eisenhower, for instance, had lied about the U-2 spy plane in 1960. President Kennedy had lied about the Bay of Pigs disaster in 1961.

66 For more information, see Herman Klurfeld, *Behind the Lines: The World of Drew Pearson* (Englewood Cliffs, NJ: Prentice-Hall, 1968); and Oliver Pilat, *Drew Pearson: An Unauthorized Biography* (New York: Harper's Magazine Press, 1973).

67 For more information, see Fred J. Cook, *Maverick: Fifty Years of Investigative Reporting* (New York: Putnam, 1984).

68 For more information, see Daniel Lewis, "Tad Szulc, 74, Dies, Times Correspondent Who Uncovered Bay of Pigs Imbroglio," *The New York Times*, May 22, 2001, p. C17; and Richard Pearson, "Tad Szulc, 74, Dies: Covered Bay of Pigs, Wrote Books," *The Washington Post*, May 22, 2001, p. B7.

As President, Johnson escalated the Vietnam War. Young people attending colleges and universities protested against the federal government. Many of the young males were opposed to being drafted into the military service. Others were protesting because of their beliefs toward the war. African Americans protested as well, but for civil rights. Even women protested because of how they were treated.[69]

When journalists started covering the escalation of the Vietnam War, they ultimately learned about atrocities committed by American soldiers. Seymour Hersh, for instance, learned about Lieutenant William L. Calley, Jr., who allegedly had been responsible for killing Vietnamese civilians in 1968. Hersh broke the story primarily because other journalists were not interested in it.[70] In fact, even though they had started writing critical stories about President Lyndon B. Johnson and his administration's policies concerning the Vietnam War, journalists mostly stayed away from covering specific incidents that could embarrass the president, his administration, and the country.

Gradually, the public's confidence in the president changed. Prominent individuals such as Dr. Martin Luther King, Jr. and Robert F. Kennedy were assassinated. Various groups grew frustrated with the lies that came from President Johnson and his administration. As a result of the negative coverage by the press, President Johnson decided not to run for reelection.

By 1970 President Richard M. Nixon was occupying the White House when several students who were protesting the war in Vietnam on the campus of Kent State University were killed by members of the National Guard. Although President Nixon was reducing the number of soldiers serving in Vietnam every month, young people, particularly those on college and university campuses, were not satisfied. When he increased bombing missions, they became outraged.

As more journalists investigated the Vietnam War, particularly those who examined classified documents from the Department of Defense, they realized officials of the government had lied to them and to the public about the war. Reporters at *The New York Times* and *The Washington Post* published numerous articles based on the Pentagon Papers, which had been leaked to them by Daniel Ellsberg. Eventually, Ellsberg was charged, but when his office was burglarized in 1971, the case against him was dismissed.[71]

69 Edd Applegate, *Political and Social Change in the United States*, 89–92, 118–119.

70 For more information, see the entry about Seymour Hersh in this book.

71 David L. Protess, et al., *The Journalism of Outrage*, 50.

In 1972 the headquarters of the Democratic National Committee, which was in the Watergate complex, was broken into. Most reporters in Washington thought the incident was nothing more than a robbery gone wrong. However, a story appearing in *The Washington Post* captured the attention of Bob Woodward and Carl Bernstein, two young reporters at the paper who investigated the break-in and the money the accused had been paid. Apparently the story had been seen by one or more reporters at *The New York Times*, too, because, like Woodward and Bernstein at *The Washington Post*, *The New York Times* had reporters investigating the break-in, the burglars, the Committee for the Reelection of the President, and other individuals. Eventually, story after story uncovered what became known as "Watergate." Besides the press, the Federal Bureau of Investigation got involved.

As mentioned, investigative journalism takes time, which is expensive. Generally, only the large metropolitan newspapers have the resources to unravel incidents like "Watergate." In fact, at the time, newspapers were hurting financially. Afternoon newspapers, particularly, were dying or being merged into other papers. The Newspaper Preservation Act of 1970, which allowed newspapers to merge operations for financial reasons, helped some newspapers, but it was not enough to save many afternoon papers.

Newspapers also had to compete against television networks that were willing to invest time and money so their news staffs could investigate the federal government and its handling of the Vietnam War or its connection to the break-in at the Watergate complex. In fact, the networks' news programs and their coverage of the hearings before the U. S. Senate caused more people to become interested in the break-in.[72]

In addition to regular evening news programs on the major networks, in 1968 Don Hewitt of CBS News was responsible for "60 Minutes," which covered various topics each week. Eventually, the program earned money for CBS, which was unheard of at the time. ABC and NBC followed with similar investigative programs.

Although President Nixon ultimately resigned from office, it was not because of the media's investigation of a few burglars. It was because of the federal government doing its own investigation and the U. S. Senate learning about misconduct by several top members of the administration. Besides, the investigative journalists investigating "Watergate" did not learn about it

72 David L. Protess, et al., *The Journalism of Outrage*, 51.

through the air. They had sources, including employees of the federal government, which provided answers to their questions.

Ultimately, many people had little trust in their federal government. This fact, perhaps more than any other, forced the press to examine its role in society. Should publishers and editors demand that every news story be objective? Should a journalist's opinions appear only in an editorial? Should more problems be thoroughly investigated?

Primarily because of the media's investigation of the Vietnam War and the break-in at the Watergate complex, investigative journalism of a national incident became popular again. No longer was this form of journalism reserved for a local or state problem.

* * *

Because the mainstream press had not performed its duties to the public well, alternative newspapers, magazines, and other media were founded in the 1960s and 1970s. Generally, these new media catered to specific groups such as young liberals, gays, and listeners of rock music, to mention a few. For instance, *Ramparts*, a magazine that was published from 1962 to 1975, included numerous muckraking articles over the years. *Rolling Stone* was founded in 1967 by Jann Wenner and focused on artists of rock and roll, investigative journalism, and, later, gonzo journalism written by Hunter S. Thompson before the magazine moved in the late 1980s. In 1970 *Scanlon's Monthly* was founded, but it lasted about a year. Gloria Steinem helped found *Ms.* magazine in 1972. The magazine, which was published every month for years, became a quarterly in the late 1980s. *Ms.* attempted to make women realize they did not have to be what men thought they should be. *Mother Jones* was founded in 1974. Although it has evolved over the years, it still includes muckraking journalism. Other publications were founded for students who attended specific colleges and universities. Young reporters at these publications were eager to investigate problems, too.

* * *

In 1975 several successful investigative journalists founded the Investigative Reporters and Editors (IRE) organization. The original purpose was to teach journalists how to research and write investigative journalism as well as to persuade aspiring investigative journalists to work collaboratively in teams. Its members are mostly journalists.[73]

73 Investigative Reporters and Editors (ire.org/about-ire/), January 12, 2022.

In 1976 members of this organization and other investigative journalists arrived in Phoenix, Arizona, to investigate the death of investigative journalist Don Bolles.

Don Bolles

Donald F. Bolles was born in Milwaukee in 1928 and graduated from Beloit College in 1950. He worked for the Associated Press (AP) from the early 1950s to the early 1960s and then became an investigative journalist for the *Arizona Republic*, a newspaper in Phoenix.

Bolles investigated several companies that were involved in schemes concerning land. He also investigated a company that owned dog and horse racing tracks in Arizona. Unfortunately, many of his articles about illegal activities were ignored by authorities. Then, in 1976, he wrote about a wholesale liquor dealer and landowner who had been interested in serving on the state racing commission that oversaw dog and horse racing. Apparently, the man did not like what Bolles had written. Eventually, Bolles received a telephone call from a man who asked the reporter to meet him at a hotel. Bolles, thinking he was about to receive important information, went to the hotel, but the man never arrived. Bolles left the hotel and drove his car out of the parking lot. Suddenly, a bomb exploded. Several days later Bolles died from his wounds.

Later, a few individuals were arrested, convicted, and sentenced. However, even though the individuals who were sentenced told about the person who had initiated the hit on Bolles, the man was not charged at the time.[74]

Investigative reporters from across the country wrote story after story, which appeared in newspapers throughout the nation.

* * *

A year later The Center for Investigative Reporting was founded. The nonprofit organization investigated numerous topics, including the Black Panthers, the FBI, nuclear accidents, consumer products, diet drugs, race relations, the coal industry, General Motors, education, and privacy issues, over the years. The reports appeared in print, on radio, on television, and on the internet.[75] The center still investigates topics. The question is whether the organization's investigations are read, heard, or viewed?

74 "Donald F. Bolles." *Gale Literature: Contemporary Authors*. Detroit: Gale, 2002.

75 Center for Investigative Reporting (Reveal) (revealnews.org), January 12, 2022.

The Center for Public Integrity, a nonprofit, was founded in 1989 for the purpose of investigating powerful interests that had betrayed the public trust. The center investigated the U. S. economy, toxic chemicals and public health, the coal industry, labor, prosecutors, the media, asbestos, medical fraud, campaign spending, the Bank of America, Congress, pesticides, airline safety, the gambling industry, the Environmental Protection Agency, the Pentagon, and the U. S. Forest Service, among other topics.[76] The center still investigates topics. The question is whether the organization's investigations are being read, heard, or viewed?

Other nonprofit organizations were founded for investigative journalism over the years.

* * *

Although publishers of large metropolitan dailies were committed to investigative journalism, by 1990 fewer were actually encouraging their editors to assign stories that would take a long time. Of course, there were a few exceptions. For instance, editors at *The Los Angeles Times*, *The New York Times*, *The Wall Street Journal*, and *The Washington Post*, among other large daily newspapers, were free to assign investigative stories that would take considerable time.

David Willman

Investigative journalist David Willman, for example, had worked for *The Los Angeles Times* before he joined *The Washington Post* in 2020.

Born on October 18, 1956, Willman graduated from San Jose State University in 1978. He worked as a reporter for *The Pasadena Star-News* from 1978 to 1983, *The San Jose Mercury News* from 1983 to 1990, and *The Los Angeles Times* from 1992 to 2020.

Willman wrote stories about local, state, and national politics. He investigated the relationship between pharmaceutical companies and scientists who worked at the United States National Institutes of Health, which led to several reforms.

In 2000 Willman wrote the series "Seven Deadly Drugs," which concerned unsafe prescription drugs that had been approved by the Food and Drug Administration, much to the chagrin of the administration's own experts.

76 Center for Public Integrity (publicintegrity.org/about/), January 12, 2022.

In 2011 his book *The Mirage Man: Bruce Ivins, the Anthrax Attacks, and America's Rush to War* was published. The book concerned the anthrax attacks that killed several individuals as well as the person responsible.

Five years later he pointed out the various problems with the nation's missile defense system, which was a cause for alarm.[77]

* * *

As more radio stations and television networks came into existence, newspapers' readerships declined. As a result, advertising revenue decreased as well. Consequently, newspapers cut staffs. Generally, reporters who wrote investigative journalism were let go before others.

Magazines, too, were suffering from a decrease in advertising revenue. However, there were several that kept investigative journalists on their staffs.

Richard Behar

For instance, Richard Behar, who had graduated from New York University in 1982, worked for *Forbes*, *Time*, and *Fortune* magazines between 1982 and 2004, and wrote numerous articles for these publications. Behar wrote lengthy exposés about the Internal Revenue Service, the World Trade Center bombing of 1993, organized crime's involvement in New York's trash collection industry, the Church of Scientology, and Donald Rumsfeld, to mention a few subjects.

In addition to his work for magazines, Behar established "Project Klebnikov" primarily to investigate the murder of Paul Klebnikov, who had been the editor-in-chief of *Forbes Russia* before his death.

In 2012 Behar returned to *Forbes* as the magazine's Contributing Editor of Investigations.

Three years later he co-founded "The Mideast Reporter" (now "Mideast Dig"), which provides investigative journalism about the Middle East.[78]

Gary Weiss

Gary Weiss was another investigative journalist who worked for magazines. Weiss earned his bachelor's from the City College of New York and his master's from Northwestern University before he worked for *Barron's* and later *Business Week*. For the latter magazine. he wrote about the American Stock Exchange,

77 "David Willman." *Gale Literature: Contemporary Authors*. Detroit: Gale, 2012.

78 "Richard Behar." *Wikipedia, The Free Encyclopedia*. 1 December 2021 (February 17, 2022); also, "www.richardbehar.com."

the Securities and Exchange Commission, Solomon Brothers, and other entities that were involved in questionable practices or illegal activities. Later, Weiss became a contributing editor for *Conde Nast Portfolio*. He also wrote a few books, including *Born to Steal: When the Mafia Hit Wall Street*, which was published in 2003; *Wall Street Versus America: The Rampant Greed and Dishonesty that Imperil Your Investments*, which was published in 2006; and *Ayn Rand Nation: The Hidden Struggle for America's Soul*, which was published in 2012.[79]

* * *

Cutting staffs at newspapers continued into the 2000s. In 2020, for instance, almost 31,000 people worked in the newspaper industry. These people included editors, reporters, photographers, film editors and operators, and video editors and operators. This figure was down twelve percent from 2019 and fifty-seven percent from 2004, according to Pew Research.[80] In other words, investigative journalists are rare at most newspapers. This is true for local radio stations, local television stations, and certain national radio and television networks.

Of course, the majority of adults get some news from news outlets online. For instance, in 2020, 32.1 million adults visited these outlets and averaged 1.95 minutes per visit, which, unfortunately, is not long enough to read an investigative story, let alone a series.[81]

Large daily newspapers that continued to do investigative journalism typically had their reporters stay away from stories about corruption that involved public officials or leaders of major corporations.[82] In short, unlike the journalists of the muckraking era, editors and their investigative journalists of the 1980s, 1990s, and 2000s were cautious about which subjects they investigated. For the most part, this is true today.

Unfortunately, this is a terrible time for the media. According to various surveys, the majority of people do not necessarily believe what they read, hear, or view. (Of course, this includes investigative journalism, which tends to include the journalist's point of view.) And the so-called news networks provide everything but news. Most of the time, each of these media provides opinions because of the medium's agenda, which is typically Left, not Center, and certainly not Right. In fact, only a few media have agendas that lean to the latter.

79 "Gary Weiss." *Gale Literature: Contemporary Authors*. Detroit: Gale, 2008.

80 Pew Research (pewresearch.org/journalism/fact-sheet/newspaper/), December 1, 2021.

81 Pew Research (pewresearch.org/journalism/fact-sheet/digital-news/), January 12, 2022.

82 Rosemary Armao, "The History of Investigative Reporting," 46.

Part II

Investigative Journalists and Writers

Henry Brooks Adams (1838–1918)

Henry Adams had a varied career, including working as a freelance journalist who exposed political corruption in the nation's capital.

Adams was born on February 16, 1838, to Abigail Brown Adams and Charles Francis Adams. The great-grandson of John Adams and the grandson of John Quincy Adams, Adams lived in Boston during the winters and in Quincy, Massachusetts, during the summers.

An avid reader, he enjoyed the works of Sir Walter Scott and Charles Dickens. He also enjoyed the volumes of history that filled the shelves of his father's library.

Adams attended Mr. Dixwell's School before he enrolled at Harvard College (University), where he was influenced by James Russell Lowell. Adams and Lowell had lengthy discussions about various subjects, including civil law.

In 1858 Adams went to Berlin, Germany, where he did postgraduate work in civil law. Within months he grew tired of studying a subject that was taught by faculty who spoke German, a language that he did not fully understand. In 1860 he toured Europe, and later wrote letters in which he described his meeting with Giuseppe Garibaldi to the *Boston Courier*.

Later that year Adams returned to Boston and then worked as his father's secretary in Washington, D.C. He enjoyed Washington, particularly the political scene.

In 1861 he returned to Boston, where he studied law until the South fired on Fort Sumter. Although his brother Charles Francis and numerous friends volunteered for the army, Adams worked as his father's secretary in London. He desired to serve in the army, however, so he asked his brother to help him get a commission. His brother refused, informing him that he was not suited for the army. Adams soon grew disillusioned with life. He was in his twenties and he did not have a career. His father persuaded him to socialize, and as a result of meeting people others only read about, his attitude changed. After completing his duties as his father's secretary, he found time to read the works of John Stuart Mill and other philosophers.

At the suggestion of John G. Palfrey, who had been editor of the *North American Review*, Adams wrote an article about Captain John Smith. The article was published in the *Review* in 1867. He contributed "British Finance in 1816" and "The Bank of England Restriction" to the magazine the same year.

In 1868 Adams returned to Washington, D.C., where he eventually investigated political corruption as a free-lance journalist for several publications, including the *North American Review* and *The Nation*.

He investigated the political differences pertaining to legal tender and wrote "The Argument in the Legal Tender Case," which *The Nation* published in 1868.

He explored finance and the political process and sent the resulting article, "American Finance, 1865–1869," to Henry Reeve, editor of the *Edinburgh Review*. The article was published in 1869 and was reprinted in the United States.

Adams examined the congressional session of 1869–1870 in a lengthy article that was sent to the *North American Review*. "The Session," the first part of the article, appeared in the April 1869 issue. The second part appeared under the title "Civil Service Reform" in the October 1869 issue. The third part, "The Session. Part II," appeared in the July 1870 issue.

With Francis A. Walker, Adams co-wrote "The Legal Tender Act," which concerned the act of 1862. For the first time in the nation's history, the federal government could print paper money. The article was published in the April 1870 issue of the *North American Review*.

Charles Adams, Henry's brother, investigated the Erie Railroad, which Cornelius Vanderbilt had tried to buy. However, Daniel Drew, Jim Fisk, and Jay Gould, learning of Vanderbilt's interest, schemed to lower and then raise the stock's value so they could buy it for very little and then sell it for a sizable profit. Drew, Fisk, and Gould basically milked the railroad out of millions of dollars.

The three set their eyes on gold, too. They schemed to corner the gold market by purchasing it, raising the price on the markets, and selling it before the price fell. In order for the scheme to succeed, they had to become friends with those in high places, which they did through Abel Rathbone Corbin who was married to President Ulysses S. Grant's sister. Of course, they offered Corbin a considerable sum. When President Grant realized what Corbin and the other three were up to, he broke off relations with Corbin. Drew, Fisk, and Gould unloaded their gold before it decreased in value.

While Charles investigated the railroad, Henry investigated the gold conspiracy and wrote a lengthy article. He offered it to Henry Reeve of the *Edinburgh Review*, but Reeve was afraid to publish it. Adams offered the article to the *Quarterly*, but the editor refused it. Finally, the editor of the *Westminster Review* accepted it.

Although Adams turned to other forms of writing, his articles were reprinted in other journals, particularly those published in the United States. Adams had called for civil service reform and the retention of the silver standard. He had revealed the power of specific monopolies such as railroads.

Adams, who had gone to London before 1870, was invited to teach history at Harvard. He returned to Boston, discussed the position with the college's president, and became a member of the faculty. In addition to teaching, he became editor of the *North American Review*.

In 1872 he married Marian Hooper of Boston, and they subsequently traveled abroad. Upon their return, Adams resumed teaching, editing the review, and writing articles. In 1876 he resigned from editing the review. Then he resigned from Harvard. In 1877 he and his wife moved to Washington, D.C., where his friends, including the statesmen William Evarts and John Hay, lived. Adams and his wife socialized with Evarts, Hay, and the geologist Clarence King, whom Adams had met several years earlier.

Adams studied the national government and wrote *The Life of Albert Gallatin*, which was published in 1879. He also edited *The Writings of Albert Gallatin*, which consisted of three volumes and was published the same year.

Adams analyzed national politics in *Democracy: An American Novel*, which was published anonymously in 1880. Madeleine Lee, the main character, moves to Washington, D.C., to experience national politics. She learns about the struggle between the newly elected president and the senator from Illinois, Silas P. Ratcliffe. Ratcliffe desires to know, use, and marry Lee. He succeeds in manipulating her and almost succeeds in marrying her, but she learns from a relative that Ratcliffe is a corrupt politician. Lee leaves Washington, D.C. and Ratcliffe. The novel became a best-seller.

In 1882 Adams wrote the biography *John Randolph* for the American Statesmen series. Adams did not find Randolph, a politician from Virginia, a congenial subject, and consequently had to borrow material from an earlier biography.

In 1884 Adams wrote *Esther*, a novel published under the pseudonym Frances Snow Compton. It was not well received by readers, and Adams turned his attention to political subjects.

Mrs. Adams, who suffered from ill health, committed suicide in 1885. Grief-stricken, her husband traveled to Japan with the painter John La Farge in 1886, primarily to escape the loneliness of his home.

When he returned home, his friends and relatives visited him often, and his attitude toward life changed. Adams worked diligently on his *History of the United States During the Administrations of Jefferson and Madison*. The first two volumes concerned the first administration of Thomas Jefferson and were published in 1889. The next four volumes covered the second administration of Jefferson and the first administration of James Madison, and were published in 1890. The last three volumes concerned the second administration of Madison and were published in 1891.

As a result of this work, Adams was considered a major American historian. His history emphasized national politics more than national economics, and it was one of the best histories of early American politics of its day.

After the last three volumes were published, Adams and La Farge visited Hawaii and Tahiti. Over the next few years Adams did very little writing. Traveling filled his time. He went to Cuba with Clarence King and to Europe with Henry Cabot Lodge and his wife. He traveled alone through Mexico. With John Hay and his wife, he visited Egypt. Although his home was in Washington, D.C., Adams frequented Paris, where he eventually lived for several months each year.

In 1895 he visited Caen, Coutances, and Mont-Saint-Michel in France. Later he wrote *Mont-Saint-Michel and Chartres*, which concerned medieval life and philosophy. The book was published privately in 1904. Requests for the book, particularly by the American Institute of Architects, caused Adams to allow the book to be published for the general public.

In 1906 Adams privately published *The Education of Henry Adams*, which was considered by readers to be an autobiography. Adams presented his opinions about various subjects, including his life.

In 1908 he assisted the widow of his friend John Hay in selecting her husband's letters for a volume that was privately published. *A Letter to American Teachers of History*, which was published in 1910, concerned the second law of thermodynamics and the historian of the future.

In 1911 Adams published a brief biography of the poet George Cabot Lodge, the son of Senator Henry Cabot Lodge, who in a sense had been his protégé.

Adams grew ill in 1912. After several months of being incapacitated, he recovered, although his vision was partially impaired. He died in Washington six years later.

Representative Works

"The Session," *North American Review*, April 1869.

"American Finance, 1865–1869," *Edinburgh Review*, April 1869.
"Civil Service Reform," *North American Review*, October 1869.
"The Legal Tender Act" (with Frances A. Walker), *North American Review*, April 1870.
"The Session. Part II," *North American Review*, July 1870.
"The New York Gold Conspiracy," *Westminster Review*, October 1870.

Further Reading

Auchincloss, Louis. *Henry Adams*. American Writers 93. University of Minnesota Pamphlets on American Writers. Minneapolis: University of Minnesota Press, 1971.
Bishop, Ferman. *Henry Adams*. Twayne's United States Authors Series 293. Boston, MA.: Twayne Publishers, 1979.
Young, James P. *Henry Adams: The Historian as Political Theorist*. Lawrence, Kansas: University Press of Kansas, 2001.

Paul Y. Anderson (1893–1938)

Paul Anderson was born on August 29, 1893, near Knoxville, Tennessee, to Elizabeth and William Anderson. Unfortunately, Anderson's father died in a work-related accident when Anderson was three years old. Anderson's mother returned to teaching, and, in order to help the family financially, Anderson delivered newspapers in his spare time.

In 1911, when Anderson was eighteen, he became a reporter for *The Knoxville Journal*. A year later he moved to *The St. Louis Times* in Missouri. In 1913 he moved to *The St. Louis Star*. Finally, in 1914 he moved to *The St. Louis Post-Dispatch*, for which he eventually covered a major race riot in East St. Louis, Illinois. Primarily because he wrote about what he observed, which included the deaths of more than a dozen African Americans, Anderson gained national attention. In fact, he was even commended for his coverage by members of the United States Congress.

Anderson worked on the newspaper's major crusade, which called for the release of political prisoners during World War I. As if his investigative reporting was not enough, he wrote editorials for the newspaper, too.

Anderson attempted to persuade O. K. Bovard, the managing editor of *The St. Louis Post-Dispatch*, to send him to Washington, D. C., to work as a correspondent, but Bovard refused. Anderson resigned from the newspaper in 1923 and moved to Washington, D.C., where he became a freelance writer. He contributed articles to various newspapers and magazines, including *The St. Louis Post-Dispatch*, *The Omaha World-Herald*, and *The Raleigh News and Observer*.

When Albert Fall, the interior secretary in President Warren G. Harding's administration, leased government land containing oil in return for Liberty Bonds, which was illegal without proper authorization, Anderson immediately covered what became known as the "Teapot Dome" scandal. Primarily because of his stories, O. K. Bovard rehired Anderson in 1924.

In Chicago two wealthy teenage boys, Nathan Leopold and Richard Loeb, abducted and murdered a young boy, Bobby Franks. Anderson was sent to cover the trial, which was covered by prominent reporters from newspapers throughout the country primarily because of readers' interest.

A year later he was sent to Dayton, Tennessee, to cover the Scopes monkey trial. A school teacher had been charged for teaching the theory of evolution, which was against one of the laws of the state because the theory of evolution contradicted the story of creation in the *Holy Bible*.

Later the same year, Anderson, along with several others, uncovered evidence that tied Federal Judge George W. English to illegal activities. As a result, English resigned.

In 1926 Anderson uncovered evidence that led to an official inside the U. S. State Department who was attempting to sow dissension between the United States and Mexico.

Later, at the urging of Bovard, Anderson revisited the "Teapot Dome" scandal and learned that several federal government officials were still participating in questionable activities with heads of oil companies. When members of the United States Congress learned about what was happening, several officials lost their jobs, paid fines, and were sentenced to prison.

In 1929 Anderson received a Pulitzer Prize for his stories. Now famous, in addition to writing for the newspaper, he contributed a regular column to *The Nation*, a magazine in which he espoused his opinions about corruption in businesses as well as the federal government. He also criticized publishers of newspapers.

In 1932 he wrote about the United States Army confronting veterans who were demonstrating in Washington, D.C., because they had not been paid their promised bonuses. Anderson witnessed veterans, their spouses, and their children basically running for their lives because of the weapons the soldiers were carrying.

Unfortunately, Anderson, like several other reporters at the time, drank too much alcohol for his own good. In fact, he was an alcoholic who allowed his need for alcohol to interfere with his work and personal life. For instance, his three marriages were failures. He was encouraged to seek help by those who worked with him, so he went to Johns Hopkins Hospital. However, he should have sought professional help years earlier.

After years of working for *The St. Louis Post-Dispatch*, Bovard, the managing editor, had had enough of Anderson's drinking, which interfered with his work, and reluctantly fired him. Anderson went to work for *The St. Louis Star-Times*. However, in 1938, he swallowed a countless number of sleeping pills and died.

Representative Work

Stories, *The Knoxville Journal*, 1911.
Stories, *The St. Louis Times*, 1912.
Stories, *The St. Louis Star*, 1913.

Stories, editorials, *The St. Louis Post-Dispatch*, 1914–1938.
Stories, *The St. Louis Star-Times*, 1938.
Column, *The Nation*, 1929–1934.

Further Reading

Freed, Fred. "Paul Y. Anderson." *Esquire* 29 (Mar. 1948).

Ganey, Terry. "The Tragic End of Paul Y. Anderson." *Gateway Journalism Review* 43.331 (Summer 2013).

Lambeth, Edmund B. "The Lost Career of Paul Y. Anderson." *Journalism Quarterly* 60.3 (Sept. 1983).

Lambeth, Edmund B. "Paul Y. Anderson." *Dictionary of Literary Biography: American Newspaper Journalists, 1926–1950, Vol. 29*. Ed. Perry J. Ashley. Detroit: Gale, 1984.

Donald L. Barlett (1936–)

Donald L. Barlett was born on July 17, 1936, to Mary and James Barlett, in DuBois, Pennsylvania.

Barlett attended the Pennsylvania State University, and from 1958 to 1961 served as an agent in the United States Army. After military service, he worked as a reporter for *The Reading* (Pennsylvania) *Times* and later *The Akron Beacon-Journal*. Then he worked as an investigative journalist for *The Cleveland Plain Dealer* and later for *The Chicago Daily News*, before he was hired in 1970 to write investigative journalism for *The Philadelphia Inquirer*.

Although Barlett was assigned to learn about the narcotics trade as well as fraudulent bankruptcies by businesses in Philadelphia, he was teamed with James B. Steele to investigate possible fraud in the Federal Housing Administration (FHA), specifically its subsidy program that had been established to help low-income people. Primarily because of the series of articles about the FHA, which earned several journalism awards, Barlett and Steele were encouraged to work together to investigate other subjects. The newspaper fully supported their investigative efforts, including their expenses.

Barlett and Steele investigated the criminal court system in Philadelphia as well as the Internal Revenue Service (IRS), among other subjects, for the newspaper. They often employed computers in uncovering information before they interviewed individuals about a story or stories.

In 1973 their series about the production and selling of oil was published as a pamphlet under the title *Oil: The Created Crisis*.

The journalists wrote *Empire: The Life, Legend, and Madness of Howard Hughes*, which was published in 1979. Barlett and Steele examined numerous files and conducted countless interviews about the man before they wrote the book, which critics claimed was one of the best biographies of Howard Hughes ever published.

In 1985 their book *Forevermore: Nuclear Waste in America* was published. Like their previous work, this book was based on sound research and exposed the nation's ineffective policies regarding how nuclear waste was stored.

Perhaps Barlett and Steele's most talked about investigative series occurred in the 1990s. Indeed, the series was expanded into three books. The first was *America: What Went Wrong?*, which was published in 1992. The second was *America: Who Really Pays the Taxes?*, which was published in 1994. And the third was *America: Who Stole the Dream?*, which was published in 1996.

These books examined the financial problems of the middle-class who paid most of the federal taxes in the United States primarily because Congress had provided loopholes for the wealthy so they would not have to pay as much. Barlett and Steele claimed the deductions, particularly those for the wealthy, should be eliminated so no taxpayer had an advantage over another. Several critics thought the journalists were naïve and did not understand the country's tax system. Other critics thought the journalists not only understood the unfair tax system but had offered a suggestion that was logical and appropriate.

In 2000 the journalists' book *The Great American Tax Dodge: How Spiraling Fraud and Avoidance are Killing Fairness, Destroying the Income Tax, and Costing You* was published. Barlett and Steele claimed tax fraud by individuals was costing the federal government almost $300 billion a year. As a result, middle-income and lower-income taxpayers were forced to pay more in order to cover the loss, which they pointed out was not fair.

Barlett and Steele stayed at *The Philadelphia Inquirer* until 1997, when they moved to *Time* as editors-at-large.

In 2004 their book *Critical Condition: How Health Care in America Became Big Business—and Bad Medicine* was published. Barlett and Steele claimed a market approach to health care was not working. The authors examined the closings of hospitals, medical mistakes, too few health care workers such as nurses, and the problems of pharmaceutical companies, which were not necessarily forthcoming when providing information about their drugs. Even though the United States had spent more on each patient than many other countries, a patient's lifespan had not increased. The journalists believed the country could do better.

Barlett and Steele moved to *Vanity Fair* in 2007.

Their next book, *The Betrayal of the American Dream*, was published in 2012. In this book, Barlett and Steele exposed how policies during the past several decades had all but destroyed the numerous opportunities for the middle-class. Instead, Congress, big business, and Wall Street had conspired to produce an elite economic class that had clamped down on the lower economic classes, particularly the middle-class.

America: What Went Wrong? The Crisis Deepens was published in 2020 and was an updated version of one of their previous bestselling books.

Representative Work

Empire: The Life, Legend, and Madness of Howard Hughes (with James B. Steele), 1979.
Forevermore: Nuclear Waste in America (with James B. Steele), 1985.
America: What Went Wrong? (with James B. Steele), 1992.
America: Who Really Pays the Taxes? (with James B. Steele), 1994.
America: Who Stole the Dream? (with James B. Steele), 1996.
The Great American Tax Dodge: How Spiraling Fraud and Avoidance Are Killing Fairness, Destroying the Income Tax, and Costing You (with James B. Steele), 2000.
Critical Condition: How Health Care in America Became Big Business—and Bad Medicine (with James B. Steele), 2004.
The Betrayal of the American Dream (with James B. Steele), 2012.
America: What Went Wrong? The Crisis Deepens (with James B. Steele), 2020.

Further Reading

Alter, Jonathan. "Two Reporters You Don't Want on Your Tail." *Newsweek* (24 Apr. 1989).
Downie, Leonard, Jr. *The New Muckrakers*. Washington, DC.: New Republic Books, 1976.
Dygert, James H. *The Investigative Journalist: Folk Heroes of a New Era*. Englewood Cliffs, NJ.: Prentice-Hall, 1976.
O'Reilly, David. "Barlett, Steele Leave Inquirer After 26 Years." *The Philadelphia Inquirer* (2 Feb. 1997).
Ponnuru, Ramesh. "Time's Terrible Two: The Perils of Barlett and Steele." *National Review* (17 July 2000).
Seelye, Katharine. "An Established Reporting Team Moves to Vanity Fair." *The New York Times* (7 Aug. 2006).

David Barstow (1963–)

Former senior writer at *The New York Times*, David Barstow was born in 1963, in Concord, Massachusetts, and attended the Medill School of Journalism at Northwestern University in Illinois. He earned a Bachelor of Science degree in 1986.

Barstow worked at several newspapers, including *The Green Bay Press-Gazette* in Wisconsin, *The Times-Union* in Rochester, New York, and *The St. Petersburg Times* in Florida, where he was a finalist for three Pulitzer Prizes.

He joined *The New York Times* in 1999 and became a member of the newspaper's investigative unit in 2002. Barstow and Lowell Bergman, another member of the unit, wrote a series of articles about various employers that had overlooked safety for their workers and consequently had been cited for safety violations. According to the journalists, these safety violations had caused deaths and injuries to hundreds of workers over the years. Barstow and Bergman received the Pulitzer Prize for Public Service in 2004. They also received a Polk Award for Labor Reporting and a Goldsmith Prize.

Barstow wrote the series "Message Machine," which concerned the Pentagon's efforts to persuade retired military officers, including generals, who were contributors to various news organizations, to put a positive spin on the wars in Iraq and Afghanistan. Barstow pointed out that a few of these individuals had ties to companies that directly benefited from such military operations. Barstow received a Polk Award for National Reporting as well as the Pulitzer Prize for Investigative Reporting in 2009.

He and another investigative journalist, Alejandra Xanic von Bertrab, wrote the series "Walmart Abroad." This series revealed the company's use of bribery in order to grow rapidly in Mexico and strangle its competition. The journalists received a Polk Award for Business Reporting, a Gerald Loeb Award, and the Pulitzer Prize for Investigative Reporting in 2013.

Along with Susanne Craig and Russ Buettner, Barstow wrote about former President Donald Trump's claims that he had become a billionaire primarily on his own. The journalists discussed several issues. For instance, they pointed out that the former president had inherited wealth from his father. Furthermore, the former president was not necessarily worth as much as he claimed. The journalists received a Polk Award for Political Reporting and the Pulitzer Prize for Explanatory Reporting in 2019.

Barstow left *The New York Times* later the same year and became the holder of the Reva and David Logan Distinguished Chair in Investigative Journalism in the Graduate School of Journalism at the University of California, Berkeley.

Representative Works

"Message Machine," *The New York Times*, 2009.
"Walmart Abroad" (with Alejandra Xanic von Bertrab), *The New York Times*, 2013.

Further Reading

(www.nytimes.com/by/david-barstow).
(www.vcresearch.berkeley.edu/faculty/david-barstow).
(www.journalism.berkeley.edu/person/david-barstow/).
www.pulitzer.org/winners/david-barstow-susanne-craig-and-russ-buettner-new-york-times).

Carl Bernstein (1944–)

Carl Bernstein and Bob Woodward uncovered a series of events that first angered President Richard Nixon and then indirectly forced him from office. Bernstein was born in 1944 and reared in Washington, D.C. His parents were members of the Communist Party during the 1940s and became active in the civil rights movement. Bernstein disliked school. When he was sixteen, he became a copy boy at *The Washington Star*, but his determination to become a reporter encouraged him to write stories about various civic meetings. He was placed on the night shift and typed stories that were called in by reporters. He also wrote obituaries from information supplied by funeral directors as well as articles based on press releases.

Eventually, he was moved to the day shift. He still typed stories that were called in by reporters, but he covered crimes, meetings, and fires at night. Although he became a member of the *Star*'s reporting staff as a summer replacement, and attended the University of Maryland part-time, he grew frustrated when he was ordered back to the dictation bank. Shortly thereafter he joined the Elizabeth, New Jersey, *Daily Journal*, for which he wrote features and a column. His colorful personal reporting of the Manhattan blackout of 1965 appeared on the *Daily Journal*'s front page and won first prize from the New Jersey Press Association.

After trying to get a job with one of New York City's dailies, he was hired by *The Washington Post* in 1966. Bernstein was assigned to various beats, including the police department, city hall, the courts, and the Virginia legislature. However, like Woodward, he also began to cover stories he thought were interesting. Indeed, his stories about the various lifestyles in and around Washington were historically sound, for he captured the milieu. Through vignettes, he allowed readers to see as well as hear the characters who gave the city its color.

Before Watergate, Bernstein also wrote several investigative stories on such topics as drug trafficking, slum landlords, fly-by-night schools, and police corruption.

Although Woodward had been assigned to cover the July 1972 burglary at the Democratic Party headquarters in the Watergate building and had written several other stories concerning Watergate, Bernstein realized that Woodward could not cover all the tips or leads alone, and persuaded the editors to let him work with Woodward. Within four months "Woodstein" had traced the money that a burglar had on him to Attorney General John Mitchell, the campaign director of the Committee to Re-Elect the President (CREEP) at the time of the break-in.

In 1974 Woodward and Bernstein's first book, *All the President's Men*, was published. It detailed how the team had investigated the various leads, describing their successes as well as failures in obtaining information for stories. The book, written in the third person for the sake of objectivity, was praised by critics for its realistic depiction of the newspaper business and its authentic record of history.

Two years later the reporters' second book, *The Final Days*, was published. Although they had intended to write of the impeachment and subsequent trial of the president from the perspective of six senators involved in the case, they had to dismiss the idea when they learned that the president would resign. Woodward and Bernstein investigated the last fifteen months of the Nixon White House. After interviewing almost 400 persons, they wrote an in-depth account of the last days. The book sold well, but several critics harshly criticized it for its disregard of historical reporting. Other critics termed the book a nonfiction novel because of its literary style and its use of anonymous sources. Many critics, however, considered the book to be an extraordinary piece of contemporary history.

Woodward stayed at the *Post*, but Bernstein resigned from the newspaper in 1977 to devote his time to freelance writing. For instance, he contributed "The CIA and the Media," an article about the cooperation between the CIA and the media during the Cold War, to *Rolling Stone* in 1977. He worked for ABC News and served as the network's Washington Bureau Chief from 1980 to 1984.

After he left ABC News, Bernstein wrote *Loyalties: A Son's Memoirs*, which was published in 1989. An autobiography, it focused on Bernstein's relationship with his father and mother during the McCarthy era. Bernstein revealed that his parents had been members of the Communist Party during the 1940s.

In 1992 he wrote an investigative article about the alliance between Pope John Paul II and President Ronald Reagan for *Time Magazine*. The same year he criticized modern journalism in the article "The Idiot Culture," which was published in *The New Republic*. With Marco Politi, he wrote *His Holiness: John Paul II and the History of Our Time*, a papal biography, which was published in 1996. Bernstein implied that the pontiff was responsible for causing the former Soviet Union to fail.

In 2005 Bernstein and Bob Woodward wrote *The Secret Man: The Story of Watergate's Deep Throat*, which was about Mark Felt, the man who had helped steer the reporters when they investigated the break-in at the Watergate complex.

In addition to articles about John McCain and Rupert Murdock, among other subjects, Bernstein wrote *A Woman in Charge: The Life of Hillary Rodham Clinton*, which was published in 2007, and *Chasing History: A Kid in the Newsroom*, which was published in 2022. The latter, another memoir, focused on his early days in newspaper journalism during the Kennedy years. Bernstein remembered the struggle for civil rights, not to mention various crimes.

Bernstein can be seen from time to time on different television programs.

Representative Works

All the President's Men (with Bob Woodward), 1974.
The Final Days (with Bob Woodward), 1976.
"The CIA and the Media," *Rolling Stone*, October 20, 1977.
"The Holy Alliance," *Time Magazine*, February 24, 1992.
"The Idiot Culture," *The New Republic*, June 8, 1992.
His Holiness: John Paul II and the History of Our Time (with Marco Politi), 1996.
The Secret Man: The Story of Watergate's Deep Throat (with Bob Woodward), 2005.

Further Reading

Adrian Havill. *Deep Truth: The Lives of Bob Woodward and Carl Bernstein*. New York: Birch Lane Press, 1993.
Carl Bernstein. *Encyclopedia of World Biography*. Vol. 29. Detroit: Gale, 2009.
Carl Bernstein. *Contemporary Authors*, Vols. 81–84. Detroit: Gale Research, 1979.
Richard Lee. "Carl Bernstein: Life after Watergate," *The Washingtonian* 16 (July 1984): 77+.
Woodward and Bernstein. *Encyclopedia of World Biography Online*. Detroit: Gale, 1998.

George William Bliss (1918–1978)

George W. Bliss not only received a Pulitzer Prize for his investigative journalism in 1962, he helped others earn Pulitzer Prizes, too.

Bliss was born on July 21, 1918, to Marie and William Bliss, in Denver, Colorado. His father was a reporter for *The Denver Post*. When he was hired as an editor by *The Chicago Herald and Examiner*, he moved the family to the outskirts of Chicago.

Bliss attended Lyons Township High School in La Grange, Illinois. After he graduated, he attended Northwestern University until he landed a job at *The Chicago Evening American*. In 1939 he was promoted to a reporter. Bliss excelled at covering topics such as labor, which he probably learned about from his father, considering his father's experience in journalism.

In 1942 Bliss joined the staff at *The Chicago Tribune*. When the United States entered World War II, he served in the United States Navy. Upon his discharge from service, he returned to the newspaper, for which he covered the police beat.

In 1951 Bliss wrote about juveniles being sexually and physically abused at a state-operated home for young people. Two years later he wrote about a couple of crime bosses who had attempted to take control of the local Teamsters Union in Chicago. Bliss and another reporter developed a chart that revealed the organization of the crime syndicate in the city.

Bliss continued to investigate organized crime. In 1961 he wrote a series of articles about organized crime and its connections to the Metropolitan Sanitary District of Greater Chicago. The series was eye-opening, to say the least. Indeed, he presented details about widespread corruption, including fraud, kickbacks, questionable contracts, and questionable hiring practices, among other criminal activities. Bliss received the Pulitzer Prize for Local Reporting—No Edition Time in 1962 for his reports.

A few years later he revealed that trucking companies headquartered in Chicago and the surrounding area had purchased licenses in other states so they would not have to pay expensive Illinois fees. Bliss was still investigating the activity, including the secretary of state for Illinois, Paul Powell, and his office which oversaw the licensing of trucks, when he was told by William Maxwell, the editor, to stop his investigation. Although Maxwell had met with Powell to discuss another matter, apparently, he had learned from Powell that Powell had not liked the reporting by Bliss.

Bliss resigned from the newspaper and went to work for the Better Government Association of Chicago. Bliss became the organization's chief investigator. In this position, he worked with investigative journalists who worked at the daily newspapers in the city. One of the first investigations he was involved in as the organization's chief investigator concerned possible collusion between officers of the Chicago Police Department and several of the city's largest private ambulance companies. Through a tip Bliss learned that a specific ambulance company was paying off officers. Bliss informed William Jones, an investigative journalist at *The Chicago Tribune*. The two participated in a staged sting operation that resulted in photographs being taken of illegal activity.

Jones wrote a series of articles about what they had uncovered, including Medicaid fraud, payoffs to officers of the police department, and even mistreatment of patients. As a result, indictments were brought against ten police officers and officials of six ambulance companies. Jones received the Pulitzer Prize for Local Investigative Specialized Reporting in 1971.

When William Maxwell retired, Bliss returned to *The Chicago Tribune* in 1971. Within a short time he was leading a team of investigative journalists. He, along with several others, investigated the Chicago Police Department, which had received hundreds of complaints for police brutality. In fact, Bliss and his team examined several hundred cases. They interviewed numerous individuals who had filed complaints. Eventually, Bliss and his team produced a series of articles about what they had learned. Indictments were brought against several police officers. The Chicago Police Department was forced to enact policies that either eliminated or at least reduced excessive force.

Bliss and his team investigated possible voter fraud in Chicago. Bliss realized that if the rumors were true, the city had a history of voter fraud going back decades. Eventually, Bliss and his team uncovered numerous individuals who had committed voter fraud. They had used different names so they could vote numerous times. The team turned the evidence over to the United States Attorney, but nothing happened. Bliss and his team continued their investigation and learned that hundreds of ballot applications had either fake names or forged names. The team's articles appeared in 1972. As a result, a federal grand jury indicted numerous election judges for fraud. Bliss and William Mullen, another investigative journalist, received the Pulitzer Prize for Local General or Spot News Reporting in 1973.

Although Bliss and his team's efforts had uncovered all sorts of criminal activity, Bliss was not finished. In 1975 he and Chuck Neubauer, another investigative journalist, investigated the Federal Housing Administration (FHA). Specifically Bliss, Neubauer, and a few others investigated the FHA's program that helped low-income people to purchase houses. Bliss and Neubauer reported that federal officials of the Department of Housing and Urban Development (HUD) had been colluding with officers of mortgage companies and that the mortgage companies had been wasting taxpayer dollars. Bliss, Neubauer, and other members of the team received the Pulitzer Prize for Local Investigative Specialized Reporting in 1976.

Bliss suffered from depression, especially after his first wife died in 1959. Although he remarried and was able to keep his depression under control, he took a leave of absence from the newspaper in late 1977 and sought medical help. He returned to the newspaper in May 1978. Unfortunately, on September 11, 1978, he shot and killed his wife and then shot and killed himself.

Representative Work

"City Sanitary District Loaded with Political Favorites," *The Chicago Tribune*, 1961.

"Police Brutality Exposed" (with others), *The Chicago Tribune*, 1973.

"Task Force Report: Reveal Huge Vote Fraud" (numerous articles with others), *The Chicago Tribune*, 1972.

"Rotten Cities Resulting from a Federal Housing Program" (with Chuck Neubauer), *The Chicago Tribune*, 1975.

Further Reading

Dygert, James H. *The Investigative Journalist: Folk Heroes of a New Era.* Englewood Cliffs, NJ.: Prentice Hall, 1976.

Fischer, Heinz Dietrich, and Erica J. Fischer. *Pulitzer Prize Archive, Part A, Reportage Journalism, Local Reporting 1947–1987; From a County Vote Fraud To a Corrupt City Council.* Vol. 3. Munchen: De Gruyter Saur, 1989.

MacDougall, A. Kent, ed. *The Press: A Critical Look from the Inside.* Princton, NJ.: Dow Jones Books, 1972.

Paul Brodeur (1931–)

Born in Boston on May 16, 1931, to Paul and Sarah Brodeur, investigative journalist Paul Brodeur graduated from Phillips Academy in 1949 and from Harvard University four years later. He served in the Counter Intelligence Corps of the United States Army for three years before he became a staff writer for *The New Yorker* in 1958. Brodeur contributed articles about Charles De Gaulle's death, Robert F. Kennedy's funeral, and Werner Heisenberg, the German physicist, to the magazine's "Talk of the Town." He also wrote several novels, including *The Stunt Man*, which was published in 1972. This work depicted a young soldier who, after deserting his regiment, became a stunt man in a film that resembled his own life.

Brodeur gained respectability as an investigative journalist when his study of the asbestos industry appeared in *The New Yorker* and then as a book in 1974. Titled *Expendable Americans*, the book focused on the dangers of asbestos fibers, which cause asbestosis, a disease that eventually kills its victim, and the refusal of executives of asbestos-producing companies to correct the problems inside their plants. Brodeur had spent six years investigating the problem and writing the book. He had learned that the relationship between business and government officials was one of cordiality. The worker's life was often overlooked by both parties.

In 1977 *The Zapping of America: Microwaves, Their Deadly Risk, and the Cover-Up* appeared. Like Brodeur's previous study, this work was based on a series of articles that had appeared in *The New Yorker*. Brodeur not only explained what microwaves were and how they were produced but pointed out that invisible microwaves could possibly kill thousands of people. Since microwaves can be found in communications systems, weapon systems, video display terminals, burglar alarm systems, microwave ovens, and automobile garage door openers, to mention a few sources, every person is exposed to them.

Brodeur exposed the ill effects of microwave radiation—from physical and mental disorders to blindness and bleeding from the eyes and ears—and he criticized the government's failure to enact legislation to control microwaves and other forms of electromagnetic radiation. Indeed, according to Brodeur, branches of the federal government such as the Department of Defense covered up certain findings by stamping them SECRET.

In *The Asbestos Hazard*, which was published in 1980, Brodeur reiterated the hazards of asbestos. Five years later he adapted a series of articles that had been published in *The New Yorker* into *Outrageous Misconduct: The Asbestos Industry on Trial*, which concerned the increased number of asbestos-disease-related lawsuits that had been filed against major corporations. The Johns-Manville Corporation was mentioned because of its attempt to stifle information about asbestos and cancer. Brodeur also revealed that company executives had tried to prohibit employees and others from suing the company. According to Brodeur, lawyers who sought outrageous sums for their clients were responsible for revealing the asbestos industry's manipulative practices and irresponsibility.

The same year, in a series of articles and later the book *Restitution: The Land Claims of the Mashpee, Passamaquoddy, and Penobscot Indians of New England*, Brodeur explored an interesting subject. It was not a subject readers would associate with him, however. After all, he was known for examining cancer-causing products, not social or minority issues.

In 1989 Brodeur's investigation into electromagnetic waves and ill health was presented in *Currents of Death: Power Lines, Computer Terminals, and the Attempt to Cover Up Their Threat to Your Health*. Brodeur reported that the federal government and the electric industry had conspired to keep certain information about electric lines and some kinds of household electronics, specifically the computer, and their harmful effects from consumers. Brodeur believed that electromagnetic fields caused cancer.

In 1993 he explored this subject again in *The Great Power-line Cover-Up: How the Utilities and the Government Are Trying to Hide the Cancer Hazard Posed by Electromagnetic Fields*. Brodeur claimed that utility company executives, government officials, and even members of the press were hiding the truth about the connection between electromagnetic fields and cancer. The book's credibility was questioned by some reviewers, but Brodeur cited study after study—at least twelve—that supported his thesis. Public officials, however, disagreed with his analysis.

Brodeur donated a few hundred boxes of papers to the New York Public Library in the early 1990s. Almost twenty years later the staff informed him that it wished to return most of the material because it could be found elsewhere. (Much of the material consisted of articles from newspapers, magazines, and other sources that Brodeur had gathered over the years.) Brodeur expressed to the staff that he wished for all of the material to remain intact because it revealed the process he employed in researching and writing investigatory articles and books. Finally, in 2014 the New York Public Library transferred the entire collection to the Howard Gotlieb Archival Research Center at Boston University.

In addition to writing investigative exposes, Brodeur taught writing at several universities, including Columbia and Harvard universities.

Representative Works

Expendable Americans, 1974.
The Zapping of America: Microwaves, Their Deadly Risk, and the Cover-Up, 1977.
The Asbestos Hazard, 1980.
Outrageous Misconduct: The Asbestos Industry on Trial, 1985.
Restitution: The Land Claims of the Mashpee, Passamaquoddy, and Penobscot Indians of New England, 1985.
Currents of Death: Power Lines, Computer Terminals, and the Attempt to Cover Up Their Threat to Your Health, 1989.
The Great Power-line Cover-Up: How the Utilities and the Government Are Trying to Hide the Cancer Hazard Posed by Electromagnetic Fields, 1993.

Further Reading

Blumberg, Peter. "Paul Brodeur's War on Electromagnetic Fields." *Washington Journalism Review* 13.1 (Jan.–Feb. 1991).
Brodeur, Paul. *Contemporary Authors*. Vols. 5–8, 1st Rev. Detroit: Gale Research, 1969.
Brodeur, Paul. *Contemporary Authors, New Revision Series*. Vol. 25. Detroit: Gale Research, 1989.
Brodeur, Paul. *Secrets: A Writer in the Cold War*. London: Faber & Faber, 1997.
Brodeur, Paul (Adrian, Jr.). *Contemporary Authors, New Revision Series*. Vol. 65. Detroit: Gale Research, 1998.
Fumento, Michael. "Shock Journalism." *Reason* 26.8 (Jan. 1995).
Granger, Morgan M. "Currents of Death: Power Lines, Computer Terminals, and the Attempt to Cover Up Their Threat to Your Health by Paul Brodeur." *Scientific American* 262.4 (Apr. 1990).
"Paul Brodeur: Historian and Crusader." *Nutrition Health Review: The Consumers' Medical Journal* 66 (1993).
Weinberg, Steven. "Reflections on a Life of Controversial Reporting." *IRE Journal* 20. 4 (July–Aug. 1997).

Julius Chambers (1850–1920)

Julius Chambers was born on November 21, 1850, to Sarabella and Joseph Chambers, in Bellefontaine, Ohio. Unfortunately, his mother died rather young and he lived primarily with his grandfather. He was introduced to printers' ink when he was eleven years old; he worked as a printer's devil for *The Bellefontaine Republican*, which was owned by his uncles.

Chambers attended Ohio Wesleyan University before he enrolled at Cornell University. It is unknown whether he worked in the university's print shop, but many young men did at the time. He co-founded the Irving Literary Society in 1869, a year before he graduated.

After college, he moved to New York City, where he pounded the pavement in search of a job with a newspaper. Finally, he was hired as a reporter for *The New York Tribune*, which was owned by Horace Greeley. After two years, in 1872, primarily because of his health, he journeyed to Minnesota, where he discovered Elk Lake. Chambers declared the lake was the starting point of the Mississippi River. As a result of his discovery, he became a Fellow of the Royal Geographical Society, and wrote numerous stories for the newspaper as well as the book *The Mississippi River and Its Wonderful Valley*, which was published in 1910.

Also in 1872 he had himself committed to the Bloomingdale Insane Asylum primarily to learn how patients were treated by the staff. After ten days he was released. Chambers wrote a series of articles about his experience. As a result, twelve patients were released primarily because they were declared sane. In addition, the administration and staff at the asylum were reorganized. Ultimately, laws pertaining to insanity were changed by the state legislature. Chambers wrote the book *A Mad World and Its People*, which was based on his articles. The book was published in 1876.

Chambers moved to *The New York Herald*, which was owned by James Gordon Bennett, Jr., in 1873. Chambers was promoted to several positions during the fifteen years he was with the paper. In 1887, for instance, the editor-in-chief was so impressed with Chambers that he sent him to Paris to launch the Paris edition of the paper.

Although Chambers was happy at the *Herald*, Joseph Pulitzer asked him to become the managing editor of *The New York World* in 1889. Chambers accepted. However, he left the paper a few years later because of other interests.

Chambers had been married more than twenty years to his wife, but he got a divorce and married a much younger woman. They lived well for the time. He contributed a regular column titled "Walks and Talks" to *The Brooklyn Daily Eagle*. In fact, he wrote the column until his death. In addition, he was one of the first journalists to teach one or more courses in journalism at Cornell University in the early 1900s, and at New York University in 1910.

Chambers always tended to do more than just work at his job. For instance, he studied law at the Law School of Columbia College (now University) in New York City. He wrote numerous short stories, novels, and plays. In fact, two of the latter were produced in New York City. He and his wife traveled.

News Hunting on Three Continents, his last book, was published posthumously in 1921. Considered by critics to be an autobiography, the book contained factual information about Chambers and bits of short stories that he had written over the years.

Chambers died in 1920.

Representative Work

A Mad World and Its People, 1876.
The Book of New York, 1912.
The Mississippi River and Its Wonderful Valley, 1910.

Further Reading

Chambers, Julius. *News Hunting on Three Continents*. New York: Mitchell Kennerley, 1921.
Chambers, Julius. *Dictionary of American Biography*. New York: Charles Scribner's Sons, 1936.
Tucher, Andie. "Why Journalism History Matters: The Gaffe, the 'Stuff,' and the Historical Imagination." *American Journalism* 31.4 (Dec. 2014).

Peter Collier (1939–2019)

Peter Collier termed himself an advocacy journalist, but he was an investigative reporter and editor at *Ramparts* for several years.

Born in Hollywood, California, in 1939, Collier received both his bachelor's and master's degrees from the University of California at Berkeley. From 1964 to 1969 he was a member of the university's English faculty, and from 1967 to 1973 he was on the staff of *Ramparts*, where he advanced from writer to editor.

He edited the books, *Crisis: A Contemporary Reader*, which was published in 1969, and *Justice Denied: The Black Man in White America*, which was published in 1970 and included articles on blacks in a white man's world by such writers as Norman Podhoretz, Kenneth B. Clark, Le Roi Jones, Ralph Ellison, Jack Newfield, Tom Wolfe, Hunter S. Thompson, Norman Mailer, Paul Goodman, W.E.B. DuBois, Richard Wright, William Bradford Huie, Martin Luther King, Jr., Claude Brown, Huey R. Newton, Tom Hayden, Malcolm X, Stokely Carmichael, and Eldridge Cleaver.

Collier contributed articles to various periodicals, including *The Progressive* and *Esquire*. He wrote the best-selling investigative and historical book *The Rockefellers: An American Dynasty* in 1976. David Horowitz was the coauthor. To say the least, the book was a comprehensive examination of the Rockefeller Empire.

In 1984 Collier and Horowitz collaborated on *The Kennedys: An American Drama*, which was loaded with anecdotal material that presented another side to the Kennedy clan. Another bestseller, the book discussed Joe Kennedy's passes at his son's weekend dates as well as the drug addiction of Bobby's son.

Three years later the authors wrote the controversial biography, *The Fords: An American Epic*. Although the authors described an American dynasty, the book was severely criticized for its lack of anecdotal material to carry it along. Some reviewers complained that it was a more retelling of history that many already knew. Other critics mentioned that the book focused on Henry Ford II, not on Henry Ford I, for too much of the book. The book revealed thorny issues such as Ford's support for the Nazis. Through the use of in-depth description, dialogue, and a colorful narrative, the authors presented an honest portrait of the individuals involved.

In 1989 Collier and Horowitz examined *Ramparts* magazine in *Destructive Generation: Second Thoughts about the Sixties* and claimed the publication's anti-establishment philosophy was wrong and the authors' conservative philosophy was correct. The authors, who had become conservative after the Vietnam War, had mentioned they supported Ronald Reagan and what he stood for. They examined the Left and were disgruntled at what it represented. The book was an indictment of the so-called "Sixties Generation."

Two years later Collier wrote *The Fondas: A Hollywood Dynasty*, which devoted too much space to Jane's successful film career, love affairs, and political naiveté and Peter's failed film career and drug experimentation and too little space to their father.

The Roosevelts: An American Saga, which was written by Collier and Horowitz, was published in 1994. The book focused on Theodore, Franklin, and Eleanor, as well as the division of the family into the Oyster Bay and Hyde Park branches. It was also about their children and grandchildren and their awkward, even estranged, relationships. The authors presented the warts of an American family.

In 1998 Collier founded Encounter Books, a conservative publishing company.

He wrote *Medal of Honor: Portraits of Valor beyond the Call of Duty*, which included photographs by Nick Del Calzo, in 2003. The book contained brief biographies of the recipients of the Medal of Honor. Collier donated all the royalties to the Congressional Medal of Honor Foundation.

Collier resigned as publisher of Encounter Books in 2005.

In 2012 he wrote *Political Woman: The Big Little Life of Jeane Kirkpatrick*. Kirkpatrick had been an academic as well as a Democrat. However, like many others who had grown disillusioned with the Democrats, she became a voice for the Republicans. She served as President Reagan's ambassador to the United Nations. To say the least, Collier's biography was revealing.

Collier died November 1, 2019. He was 80 years old.

Representative Works

Crisis: A Contemporary Reader, 1969.
Justice Denied: The Black Man in White America, 1970.
The Rockefellers: An American Dynasty (with David Horowitz), 1976.
The Kennedys: An American Drama (with David Horowitz), 1984.
The Fords: An American Epic (with David Horowitz), 1987.
Destructive Generation: Second Thoughts About the Sixties (with David Horowitz), 1989.
The Fondas: A Hollywood Dynasty, 1991.
The Roosevelts: An American Saga (with David Horowitz), 1994.
Political Woman: The Big Little Life of Jeane Kirkpatrick, 2012.

Further Reading

Collier, Peter. *Contemporary Authors*. Vols. 65–68. Detroit: Gale Research, 1977.

Collier, Peter. *Contemporary Authors*, *New Revision Series*. Vol. 44. Detroit: Gale Research, 1994.

Collier, Peter. "Life along the "Ramparts."" *New Criterion* 28.5 (January, 2010).

Genzlinger, Neil. "Peter Collier, 80, a Voice of the Left, Then the Right." *The New York Times* (10 Nov. 2019).

Kimball, Roger. "Two Encounters with Reformed Radical Peter Collier: He exposed CIA Funding of a Magazine in the '60s and ran a Book Publisher of the same name in the '90s." *Wall Street Journal-Online Edition* (16 Nov. 2019).

Morrison, Micah. "Rebels with a Cause." *Insight on the News* 8.21 (25 May 1992).

Geoffrey Cowan (1942–)

Geoffrey Cowan was born May 8, 1942, in Chicago and was educated at Harvard and Yale universities, where he earned his bachelor's and law degrees, respectively.

From 1969 to 1972 Cowan worked as an attorney at the Center for Law and Social Policy in California. Then he taught law for two years as an adjunct professor at the University of California, Los Angeles. In 1974 he became a lecturer of communications at the same university.

Two years later he worked as an attorney at the Center for Law in the Public Interest, also in California.

Besides his work as a lawyer and lecturer, Cowan contributed a column to *The Village Voice*, and, with Judith Colburn, wrote an expose on Operation Phoenix, a top-secret CIA and army intelligence operation that trained counterinsurgency teams to torture and assassinate members of certain groups. Cowan and Colburn's efforts were favorably reviewed by those working in the print and broadcast media.

In 1979 Cowan wrote *See No Evil: The Backstage Battle Over Sex and Violence on Television*, another insightful piece of investigative journalism. From 1979 to 1984 he was a member of the Board of Directors of the Corporation for Public Broadcasting.

With Leroy Aarons, Cowan co-wrote the play "Top Secret: The Battle for the Pentagon Papers," which was produced in 1991 on National Public Radio. It was presented off-Broadway during the 2010 season.

His book *The People v. Clarence Darrow: The Bribery Trial of America's Greatest Lawyer* was published in 1993 and concerned Clarence Darrow, who was hired by Samuel Gompers, the president of the American Federation of Labor, to defend James McNamara and his brother John McNamara, who were arrested for the explosion that wrecked the building in which *The Los Angeles Times*, an aggressively anti-union newspaper, was housed. The case was airtight, however, and Darrow lost. The McNamaras changed their plea to guilty and consequently were sentenced to prison. Darrow was charged for attempted bribery of two jurors and had to defend himself.

Cowan served as dean of the Annenberg School for Communication and Journalism at the University of Southern California from 1996 to 2007. In 2007 he became a university professor and held the Annenberg Family Chair in Communication Leadership. He founded the Annenberg Center on Communication Leadership and Policy at the university.

From 2010 to 2016 he served as the first president of the Annenberg Foundation Trust at Sunnylands.

His book *Let the People Rule: Theodore Roosevelt and the Birth of the Presidential Primary* was published in 2016.

Representative Works

"The Seat of Government," *Village Voice*, 1969–1972.
See No Evil: The Backstage Battle Over Sex and Violence on Television, 1979.

Further Reading

Blumenthal, Sidney. "The Voice of the V.O.A." *New Yorker* 71 (18 Sept. 1995).
Cowan, Geoffrey. *Contemporary Authors*. Vols. 97–100. Detroit: Gale Research, 1981.

Helen Cusach ("Nell Nelson") (1860–1945)

Helen Cusach was born in Missouri. She moved to Chicago, where she worked as a school teacher and wrote articles for the city's newspapers. In 1888 Charles Chapin, the editor of *The Chicago Times*, offered her a job as a reporter. Chapin was interested in having Cusach find employment in factories and so-called sweatshops and write articles about her experiences.

Nelson walked all over Chicago in order to find one brief job after another. Each story appeared under the series headline, "City Slave Girls," and was written by "Nell Nelson," the pseudonym Cusach used. After her stories had been promoted on the front page of the newspaper, readers started reading her stories with interest. As they read about the horrible conditions in which employees had to work, not to mention how they were mistreated, readers grew outraged. As a result of reader interest, the newspaper's circulation increased.

Nelson's stories were matter-of-fact. She did not hold anything back. She wrote about how she tried to find work. She explained how she obtained a job. She discussed what she saw and experienced. She emphasized the poor working conditions and low wages. Generally, she wrote about a different job experience in each story. In several articles, in addition to providing her experiences, she included information from interviews with others. She included how some employees were mistreated and even cheated out of their income. She interviewed young girls who had to pay a few dollars to the prospective employer in order to be trained for a possible job. This practice was typical at numerous companies, particularly those that produced products made from cloth. She interviewed young boys, too, who were often taken advantage of by their employers. (Laws regarding young girls and boys working outside the home had not necessarily been enacted by local, state, or the federal government. Consequently, young girls and boys were abused in the workplace. In fact, many had to work long hours for very low pay.)

By the time the series ended, Nelson had worked at numerous different jobs in factories and so-called sweatshops. She had learned that many jobs for young women and boys were horrible. As a result of the series, Nelson had become popular among readers. The series, too, had become popular, so much so that the Barkley Publishing Company published the series as a book in late 1888.

Nelson moved to New York City primarily to write a similar series for *The New York World*. Although she was not directly involved, Nelson's series was partly responsible for the founding of the Illinois Woman's Alliance as well as other organizations that soon appeared across the country. These organizations were founded for the purpose of protecting young women and men from being exploited by employers by calling for educational reform, which ultimately would force children to get an education.

Nelson's first article for *The New York World* appeared under the heading "White Slave Girls." Nelson wrote about her experience working at a manufacturing company that produced novelties. She described the horrible working conditions as well as the extremely low wages. Other similar articles followed. Later, the editors of the newspaper sent her abroad to write about working conditions for women in France and Germany.

Nelson married Solomon Carvalho in 1895. Carvalho basically oversaw Joseph Pulitzer's *The New York World*. A year later Carvalho accepted an executive position with the William Randolph Hearst organization and soon became responsible for several magazines. As a result of marrying Carvalho, Nelson left journalism and started a family. They lived comfortably, had two children, and raised horses.

Although several female "stunt" journalists like Nellie Bly became famous, Nelson was often overlooked. She died in 1945.

Representative Works

"City Slave Girls of Chicago" series, *The Chicago Times*, 1888.
The White Slave Girls of Chicago, 1888.
"White Slave Girls of New York" series, *The New York World*, 1888.

Further Reading

Chapin, C. E. *Charles Chapin's Story: Written in Sing Sing Prison*. New York: G. P. Putnam's Sons, 1920.

Liguori, Eric W. "Nell Nelson and *The Chicago Times* 'City slave girls' Series: Beginning a National Crusade for Labor Reform in the Late 1800s." *Journal of Management History* 18.1 (2012).

Morris, James McGrath. *The Rose Man of Sing Sing*. New York: Fordham University Press, 2003.

Peko, Samantha, and Michael S. Sweeney. "Nell Nelson's Undercover Reporting." *American Journalism* 34.4 (2017).

Bill Dedman (1960–)

Bill Dedman was born in 1960 in Chattanooga, Tennessee, and worked as a copy boy at *The Chattanooga Times* before he graduated from high school. He attended Washington University in St. Louis, Missouri, and worked part time for *The St. Louis Post-Dispatch*. Primarily because he enjoyed journalism, he left college to work full time as a reporter for the *Warrensburg Star-Journal* and then as a reporter for the *Blue Springs Examiner*, both in Missouri.

Gaining valuable journalism experience, Dedman returned to Tennessee and worked as a reporter for *The Chattanooga News-Free Press*, *The Chattanooga Times*, and the *Knoxville News Sentinel*.

In 1987 he moved to *The Atlanta Journal-Constitution*, for which he wrote the series "The Color of Money" in 1988. Dedman used public records and accounts to learn how banks, mortgage companies, and savings and loan associations discriminated against middle-class African Americans when they were looking for loans to purchase houses. As a result, Dedman earned a Pulitzer Prize for Investigative Reporting a year later. The series was responsible for major legislative reforms, including the expansion of the federal Home Mortgage Disclosure Act by Congress.

Dedman moved to *The Washington Post* in 1989 and worked as the metropolitan reporter. One of the series he co-wrote concerned a Roman Catholic priest who allegedly had sexually abused several parishioners. The series discussed the priest, the allegations against him, and the attempted cover-up.

In 1991 Dedman worked as a freelance writer and a year later he taught journalism at the University of Maryland.

In 1994 he became the Director of Computer Assisted Reporting for the Associated Press. Although Dedman had employed computers to help him in his investigations, many reporters had not. Consequently, the Associated Press, in its efforts to help its reporters broaden their investigative skills, created this position.

Dedman moved to *The New York Times* in 1997 and wrote investigative journalism. He also wrote about baseball, particularly about the players who seemed to hit homeruns in each game.

In the early 2000s he worked as a correspondent for *The Boston Globe*. He contributed a major series about racial profiling of drivers throughout the state by the police. In essence, Dedman revealed that the police generally gave warnings to white and female drivers while they gave tickets to members of minorities and males for the same offences.

Dedman joined NBC News, including its online outlet, as an investigative journalist in 2006. He wrote about military officers who attempted to stop interrogations of detainees at Guantanamo Bay, faulty firefighting equipment that had been responsible for the deaths of firefighters, the Pentagon's seemingly lack of interest in identifying soldiers who had been killed in past wars, officials' lack of interest in inspecting bridges, officials' lack of interest in earthquakes and the possible damage such would cause to nuclear power plants, the hidden logs of visitors at the White House during Barack Obama's presidency, the White House's request to suppress Hillary Clinton's college thesis, and journalists' contributions to political campaigns, among other subjects.

One of his reports concerned Huguette Clark, a copper heiress who owned several mansions as well as other property. Instead of living in one of her properties, however, Clark had moved to a hospital room and had become a recluse. The reports were so successful that he and Paul Clark Newell, Jr., co-wrote *Empty Mansions: The Mysterious Life of Huguette Clark and the Spending of a Great American Fortune*, which was published in 2013. The book concerned not only Huguette Clark, but her father, William Clark, an industrialist who had amassed a sizable fortune before his death.

Dedman joined *Newsday* in 2014. One of the major series he and several other reporters worked on was "Long Island Divided," which appeared in the newspaper in 2019 and revealed that real estate agencies basically steered white prospective home buyers to white neighborhoods and minority prospective home buyers to minority neighborhoods.

Dedman's "Power Reporting," which provides information about him and his career, can be found on the web.

Representative Works

"The Color of Money," *The Atlanta Journal-Constitution*, 1988.

Empty Mansions: The Mysterious Life of Huguette Clark and the Spending of a Great American Fortune (with Paul Clark Newell, Jr.), 2013.

"Long Island Divided," *Newsday*, 2019.

Further Reading

Brennan, Elizabeth A., and Elizabeth C. Clarage. *Who's Who of Pulitzer Prize Winners*. Santa Barbara, California: ABC-CLIO, Inc., 1998.

Dedman, Bill. *Gale Literature: Contemporary Authors*. Detroit: Gale, 2014.

(powerreporting.com), March 8, 2022.

Ovid Demaris (1919–1998)

Ovid Demaris was born on September 6, 1919, in Biddeford, Maine, to Ernest and Aurore Demarais (Demaris changed the spelling of his birth name), and served in the United States Army Air Force before attending the College of Idaho, from which he received his bachelor's degree in 1948, and Boston University, from which he received his master's degree in 1950.

Demaris worked as a reporter for the *Quincy Patriot Ledger* in Quincy, Massachusetts, and then for the United Press in Boston. In 1953 he moved to Los Angeles, where he worked for *The Los Angeles Times*. After six years of working on the advertising staff, he resigned primarily because he was interested in investigating and writing about various subjects. He wrote magazine and book-length investigative exposes that thoroughly covered such topics as the Mafia, kidnapping, political corruption, crime in America, the links between corporations and politics, and international terrorist groups and organizations.

With Ed Reid, Demaris co-wrote *The Green Felt Jungle*, which was published in 1963. The book concerned the Mafia, prostitution, and the corrupt politicians of Las Vegas.

His book *Dirty Business: The Corporate-Political Money-Power Game*, which concerned corporations funneling money to politicians, was published in 1974. The book contained a simple, direct, and extremely forceful style of writing. His form of investigative journalism was exciting. It seemed to grab readers by the lapels and shake them.

Demaris also wrote biographires of John Dillinger, Jack Ruby, and J. Edgar Hoover, among other figures. In 1981 he wrote *The Last Mafioso: The Treacherous World of Jimmy Frantianno*, which was based on numerous interviews with Frantianno, a member of the Mafia. In addition to the interviews, Demaris had obtained a few thousand pages of actual conversations and several hundred surveillance reports from authorities, including the Federal Bureau of Investigation (FBI). The book became a bestseller.

In 1986 Demaris wrote *The Boardwalk Jungle*, which examined the arrival as well as the aftermath of legalized casino gambling in Atlantic City. Demaris had learned about the hotels, politicians, and Mafia, and had described in detail how elected officials had been corrupted by members of the Mafia.

Demaris also wrote several novels, including *Ricochet*, which was published in 1989.

His biography of J. Edgar Hoover was reissued in 1993 under the title *J. Edgar Hoover: As They Knew Him*. Demaris used personal interviews to piece together a scandalous portrait of the former chief of the FBI.

Demaris died March 12, 1998.

Representative Works

Lucky Luciano, 1960.
The Lindbergh Kidnapping Case, 1961.
The Dillinger Story, 1961.
The Green Felt Jungle (with Ed Reid), 1963.
Jack Ruby (with Garry Wills), 1968.
Dirty Business: The Corporate-Political Money-Power Game, 1974.
The Director: An Oral History of J. Edgar Hoover, 1975.
The Last Mafioso: The Treacherous World of Jimmy Fratianno, 1981.
The Boardwalk Jungle, 1986.
J. Edgar Hoover: As They Knew Him (reprint with new title), 1993.

Further Reading

"Author Yields on Order in Penthouse Libel Case." *The New York Times* 131 (14 Jan. 1982).
Desmarais, Ovid E. *Gale Literature: Contemporary Authors*. Detroit: Gale, 2007.
"Interview Tapes Sought for Trial: Author Refuses to Give Court the Material Rejected in Penthouse Libel Case." *The New York Times* 131 (6 Jan. 1982).
McDowell, Edwin. "Ovid Demaris." *The New York Times* 130 (1 Mar. 1981).

Karen Dillon (1952–)

Born in 1952 in Missouri, Karen Dillon worked as a typesetter at the *Boone News-Republican* in Iowa before she became an award-winning investigative reporter. She was a freelancer for the *Kansas City Times* when she attended the University of Missouri, from which she received a bachelor's degree in 1988 and a master's degree a year later.

After college, she worked as a reporter for the *Sarasota Herald-Tribune* for almost two years. She wrote about the arrest of Pee Wee Herman. She also investigated the police department and learned that officers, in order to arrest prostitutes for prostitution, had removed their clothing, too.[1]

Dillon moved to *The Kansas City Star* and investigated the city's police department. She learned that it had a slush fund amounting to millions of dollars. She learned that some of the money had been used for various activities, including protecting officers and even trips.[2]

In 1997 Dillon contributed to the five-part series "Money Game: Inside the NCAA." In fact, she wrote the lengthy "NCAA Certification program does little to improve gender equity." This article concerned the NCAA's efforts to correct the unequal treatment female athletes had received at colleges and universities over the years. However, Dillon learned that the NCAA had certified various programs that had not necessarily met Title IX standards and that the NCAA was behind in its certification efforts.

Four years later she wrote "To Protect and Collect," a series that examined the practices of police departments when they made drug busts. If money was seized, some departments turned the money over to the federal Drug Enforcement Administration, which, in turn, returned some eighty percent of the money to the departments. Dillon learned that many police departments did not turn the money over to the federal agency whatsoever. For this effort, Dillon received the Goldsmith Prize for Investigative Reporting in 2001.

Primarily because *The Kansas City Star* was cutting its staff, Dillon left the newspaper in 2013. She freelanced for the NBC affiliate television station, KSHB, and contributed to the documentary, "The Dark State: Lack of open records presents complete picture of many Kansas criminal cases," which was broadcast by the station in 2014. The documentary concerned the state of

1 "Karen Dillon," *Columbia Journalism Review*, Vol. 40, No. 1 (May/June 2001), 56.

2 "Karen Dillon," *Columbia Journalism Review*, Vol. 40, No. 1 (May/June 2001), 56.

Missouri's closed records law pertaining to police search warrant and arrest reports.

She also freelanced for *The Pitch*, an alternative publication in Kansas City, and wrote "Cop Donald Hubbard said he had no choice when he shot and killed firefighter Anthony Bruno last fall. That's because he'd already made some bad decisions." This lengthy article concerned a Kansas City police officer who, during his off-duty hours, had worked as a security guard at a hotel when he had been made aware of a disturbance. Apparently, the firefighter had been drinking, had argued with a taxi driver about a fare, had punched the driver, and had left. The guard had followed the firefighter, they had fought, and the guard had shot the firefighter, killing him. Dillon learned that the guard had not followed the police department's policies that applied to police officers, including those who worked as security guards during their off-duty hours.

Dillon wrote another lengthy investigative piece for *The Pitch*. Published in 2016 and titled "Prison Broke: The Missouri Department of Corrections can't escape its own worst habits," the article focused on numerous lawsuits that had been brought against the department by former personnel. These individuals had endured sexual comments, groping, threats, and even assaults by other personnel. The lawsuits had cost the state millions of dollars.

Dillon worked as an investigative journalist for the *Lawrence Journal-World* for almost two years. Then she became a freelance investigative journalist. In fact, information about her can be found at "More Than a-Matter," which is online.

In 2018 Dillon contributed "In dealing with the Ogallala Aquifer, western Kansas is running out of water and time" to *The Journal*, a publication of the Kansas Leadership Center. In this lengthy article, which was broken into chapters, she explored how the Ogallala Aquifer had provided water for farming and other uses over the years. However, primarily because more people had used the water for more needs for many years, the Ogallala Aquifer had less water. Dillon discussed the conservation efforts of farmers and others who had realized that only conservation would preserve the aquifer. The article earned two journalism awards in 2019.

Representative Works

"NCAA Certification program does little to improve gender equity," *The Kansas City Star*, 1997.

"To Protect and Collect," *The Kansas City Star*, 2001.

"The Dark State: Lack of open records presents complete picture of many Kansas criminal cases," KSHB, 2014.

"Prison Broke: The Missouri Department of Corrections can't escape its own worst Habits," *The Pitch*, 2016.

"In dealing with the Ogallala Aquifer, western Kansas is running out of water and time," *The Journal*, 2018.

Further Reading

"Karen Dillon." *Columbia Journalism Review* 40.1 (May–June 2001).

"More Than a-Matter," (www.morethanamatter.pressfolios.com).

Raymond Dirks (1934–)

Born in 1934 in Fort Wayne, Indiana, Raymond Dirks attended DePauw University, from which he graduated in 1955.

Dirks worked as an insurance analyst and later as a vice president at several firms, including Bankers Trust, Goldman, Sachs and Company, G. A. Saxton and Company, Dirks Brothers Limited, and Delafield Childs, Inc., which purchased Dirks Brothers Limited, in New York City.

He earned the reputation of being an ethical and hard-working executive. Because of this reputation, a former employee of Equity Funding Corporation of America informed him that certain officials of the corporation had falsified records, created counterfeit insurance policies, and funneled millions of dollars into fraudulent assets. Of course, Dirks did not know whether the former employee was just disgruntled or whether the accusations against the insurance company were true. He met with others who had worked at Equity Funding and they confirmed the allegations. Dirks informed institutions that held large blocks of Equity Funding stock, and the institutions sold it. Within a brief period, the insurance company was bankrupt.

In the book *The Great Wall Street Scandal*, which was written with Leonard Gross and published in 1974, Dirks explained his role in the downfall of the Equity Funding Corporation. Dirks admitted that when he learned about the scheme, he decided not to inform the authorities because an investigation would have taken too long, and if Equity Funding Corporation executives had found out about it they would have had time to cover it up. As he explained, he took it upon himself to expose the fraud, which caused Equity Funding's stock to plummet in value.

Dirks succeeded in exposing illegal activity by certain officials, but he was accused by members of the New York Stock Exchange and the Securities and Exchange Commission of spreading rumors for personal profit. Dirks persevered against these accusations, however, and the case was brought before the U.S. Supreme Court in 1983. The decision, which became known as the Dirks Decision, was for Dirks. Later, he was recognized as having performed a public service.

Dirks wrote the informative *Heads You Win, Tails You Win: The Dirks Investment Formula*, which was a guide on how to invest in stocks. The book was published in 1979.

Over the years Dirks expanded his research of the stock market. He examined healthcare stocks as well as heavily shorted stocks. As a result, he became known as the founder and principal researcher of the ShortBusters Club.

Representative Works

The Great Wall Street Scandal (with Leonard Gross), 1974.

Further Reading

"A Victory for Ray Dirks." *Dun's Business Month* 122 (Aug. 1983).
Dirks, Raymond L. *Contemporary Authors*. Vol. 106. Detroit: Gale Research, 1982.
Dirks, Raymond L. *Gale Literature: Contemporary Authors*. Detroit: Gale, 2010.
Egan, Jack. "Riding the Roller Coaster with Ray Dirks." *New York* 14 (24 Aug. 1981).
Flaherty, Robert J. "Ray Dirks—an American Legend." *Equities Magazine* 42.5 (May 1994).
"Ray Dirks Gets His Day in Court." *Business Week* (21 Mar. 1983).
Weiss, Gary. "A Dark Side to Ray Dirks?" *Business Week* (11 July 1994).
Weiss, Gary. "Blowing the Whistle on a Famous Whistle-Blower." *Business Week* (1 Aug. 1994).

Ronnie Dugger (1930–)

Investigative journalist Ronnie Dugger was born on April 16, 1930, in Chicago to William and Mary Dugger. He was educated at the University of Texas at Austin, from which he received his bachelor's degree in 1950, and Oxford University.

Dugger worked as a newscaster and sports announcer before he joined the *San Antonio Express*. Later, he broadened his experience in journalism when he wrote political copy for the International News Service and served as a foreign correspondent for several Texas newspapers.

In 1954, after he had returned from Oxford, Dugger was offered full control of the newly developed weekly, the *Texas Observer*. The newspaper had been founded to serve as an alternative to the conservative metropolitan newspapers published in Austin, Dallas, Fort Worth, and Houston.

Dugger recruited such journalists as Willie Morris, Robert Sherrill, and Larry L. King, and made the *Observer* one of the most insightful newspapers published in Texas. Indeed, the *Observer* provided in-depth political coverage as well as critical analysis of bills before the state legislature. Dugger was also a first-rate muckraker. He and his sparse staff uncovered corruption among Texas legislators as well as lobbyists. From state officials taking gifts and bribes to huge oil companies dodging taxes and polluting the environment, Dugger and his staff informed readers of the ills of Texas politicians and big business. The paper reported on Billy Sol Estes, the inhumane conditions in state mental hospitals, and the abuse of power at the University of Texas at Austin. Nothing was sacred, or so it seemed to the powerful who controlled or desired to control the state.

Although Dugger served as the newspaper's editor, editor-at-large, and publisher, he, like Morris, Sherrill, and King, resigned in the 1960s. He contributed exposes to various magazines, including *The Atlantic Monthly*, *Harper's Magazine*, *The Nation*, *The New Yorker*, and *The Progressive*. He also wrote several books, including the controversial *Our Invaded Universities: Form, Reform, and New Starts*, which was published in 1974 and argued that colleges and universities had, because of their preponderant bureaucratic structures, become institutions that promoted capitalism and demoted any or all ideas to the contrary.

The *Texas Observer* continued under the guidance of Greg Olds, followed by Kay Northcott. Molly Ivins joined Northcott in 1970. Dugger returned to the newspaper as publisher several years later, and Joe Holley became editor. Although the paper required much of his time, Dugger wrote *The Politician: The Life and Times of Lyndon Johnson; the Drive for Power, from the Frontier to Master of the Senate* in 1982, which was a critical biography that traced Johnson's greed and crudeness from his early years to his rise in politics. The book was based on extensive research, including interviews Dugger had conducted with Johnson in 1967 and 1968. The book also interpreted the effects of Johnson's policies on American and world politics. Most reviewers applauded Dugger's efforts, even though a few acknowledged it was apparent he did not like his subject.

Dugger wrote *On Reagan: The Man and His Presidency* in 1983, which examined the political philosophy that had guided Reagan's first term as president.

Dugger continued to serve as publisher of the *Texas Observer* until 1994.

A year later he wrote "A Call for Citizens: Will Real Populists Please Stand Up," which was printed in *The Nation*. The essay asked progressives to join together to recover populism from conservative politicians. As a result, the Alliance for Democracy was founded in 1996.

In 2011 Dugger received a George Polk Award for his long career in journalism.

Representative Works

Texas Observer (Publisher).

Our Invaded Universities: Form, Reform, and New Starts, 1974.

The Politician: The Life and Times of Lyndon Johnson; the Drive for Power, from the Frontier to Master of the Senate, 1982.

On Reagan: The Man and His Presidency, 1983.

Further Reading

Dugger, Ronnie. *Contemporary Authors*. Vols. 21–24, 1st Rev. Detroit: Gale Research, 1977.

Dugger, Ronnie. *Contemporary Authors, New Revision Series*. Vol. 12. Detroit: Gale Research, 1984.

Getlin, Josh. "Texas Observer No More; Tired of Politics as Usual, Groundbreaking Lone Star Journalist Ronnie Dugger Turns Organizer by Helping to Launch the Alliance For Democracy." *Los Angeles Times* 116 (18 May 1997).

Holley, Joe. "A Mid-Life Crisis in Texas." *Columbia Journalism Review* 33.5 (Jan.–Feb. 1995).

Edward Jay Epstein (1935–)

Edward Jay Epstein was born on December 6, 1935, to Betty and Louis Epstein, in New York, New York. He earned his bachelor's and master's degrees from Cornell University in 1957 and 1966, respectively, and his doctorate from Harvard University in 1973.

Epstein taught courses in political science at Harvard University, the Massachusetts Institute of Technology, and the University of California, Los Angeles. However, he is known more for his investigative journalism than for his teaching. Indeed, he has written articles for numerous publications, including *Esquire*, *Public Interest*, *Commentary*, *Reader's Digest*, *New York*, *Psychology Today*, *The New York Times Magazine*, *The New Republic*, *Columbia Journalism Review*, *The Atlantic Monthly*, *Harper's Magazine*, *Vogue*, *The New Yorker*, *The Nation*, *The New York Review of Books*, *Adweek*, *The New Criterion*, and *Newsweek*, among others.

In addition to articles, Epstein has written several books. For instance, *Inquest: The Warren Commission and the Establishment of Truth* was his first book and was published in 1966. It concerned the government body that investigated the assassination of President John F. Kennedy. Epstein revealed that the Warren Commission's purpose was to end the public's belief that more than one person had been involved in the president's assassination. In essence, according to the report, only on person had been responsible for the act.

In 1969 *Counterplot* was published. In this book Epstein examined District Attorney James Garrison's claims about Lee Harvey Oswald being connected to a small group of men in New Orleans and that he was present when the group had discussed assassinating the president. In essence, Garrison claimed more than one person had been involved in what had happened in Dallas, Texas.

Epstein wrote *News from Nowhere: Television and the News*, which was published in 1973. In this book Epstein discussed the evening news programs of ABC, NBC, and CBS. He specifically pointed out the problems of each. Two years later *Between Fact and Fiction: The Problems of Journalism* was published. This book was a collection of essays about modern journalism, including its various problems such as meeting deadlines, cutting stories because of space or time, presenting only partial truths, and/or slanting stories or playing up particular angles.

Agency of Fear: Opiates and Political Power in America was published in 1977. In this book Epstein examined President Richard Nixon's war on drugs, specifically the Office of Drug Abuse and Law Enforcement, and claimed the former president had inflated the numbers of those abusing drugs in order to establish the office.

A year later Epstein concentrated on a familiar subject, Lee Harvey Oswald, in *Legend: The Secret World of Lee Harvey Oswald.* In this book he attempted to reveal the real Lee Harvey Oswald, not the so-called "lone gunman" many people had read about in various articles and books. Epstein interviewed numerous individuals and read countless documents that had been developed by the Federal Bureau of Investigation (FBI) and the Central Intelligence Agency (CIA).

The Rise and Fall of Diamonds: The Shattering of a Brilliant Illusion was published in 1982. Epstein explored the world of De Beers Consolidated Mines Limited of South Africa, which monopolized the selling of diamonds all over the world.

Deception: The Invisible War between the KGB and the CIA was published in 1989. In this book Epstein claimed the KGB of the former Soviet Union had attempted to mislead the intelligence gathering services of the United States since the late 1950s, after the Cold War had started. In fact, the KGB had deceived these intelligence gathering services about the strengths and intentions of the former Soviet Union. As a result, the KGB had controlled or manipulated the strategic planners of the United States during the Cold War.

In 1996 *Dossier: The Secret History of Armand Hammer* was published. Epstein had access to various resources, not to mention interviews with individuals who knew Dr. Armand Hammer, the chair of Occidental Petroleum, before he died in 1990. Although Hammer had been well respected by many prominent individuals both stateside and abroad, Epstein revealed that Hammer had made a fortune by doing business with the former Soviet Union. He also claimed Hammer had been involved in espionage for the communists.

The Big Picture: The New Logic of Money and Power in Hollywood was published in 2005. In this book Epstein examined the film industry over several decades. Five years later *The Hollywood Economist: The Hidden Financial Reality behind the Movies* was published. Like the previous book mentioned, this one looked at Hollywood, too, including how the film industry employed advertising to target audiences such as teenagers.

In 2017 *How America Lost Its Secrets: Edward Snowden, the Man and the Theft* was published. Epstein revealed who Edward Snowden was at the time he stole countless documents while working as an IT analyst for the National Security Administration (NSA). In addition, he warned the federal government about employing contractors instead of full-time people and placing them in situations where they have access to sensitive or classified material.

Representative Work

Inquest: The Warren Commission and the Establishment of Truth, 1966.
Counterplot, 1969.
News from Nowhere: Television and the News, 1973.
Between Fact and Fiction: The Problems of Journalism, 1975.
Agency of Fear: Opiates and Political Power in America, 1977.
Legend: The Secret World of Lee Harvey Oswald, 1978.
The Rise and Fall of Diamonds: The Shattering of a Billiant Illusion, 1982.
Deception: The Invisible War between the KGB and the CIA, 1989.
Dossier: The Secret History of Armand Hammer, 1996.
The Big Picture: The New Logic of Money and Power in Hollywood, 2005.
The Hollywood Economist: The Hidden Financial Reality behind the Movies, 2010.
How America Lost Its Secrets: Edward Snowden, the Man and the Theft, 2017.

Further Reading

Cockburn, Alexander. "The Epstein Interrogatory." *The Nation* 251.4 (30 July 1990).
Edward Jay Epstein. *Gale Literature: Contemporary Authors*. Detroit: Gale, 2014.
Lang, Brent. " 'Hall of Mirrors': Edward Jay Epstein on the Trail of Edward Snowden." *Variety* (16 Oct. 2017). www.edjayepstein.blogspot.com (19 Feb. 2022).

Joseph C. Goulden (1934–)

Joseph C. Goulden was born to Joseph and Lecta Goulden on May 23, 1934, in Marshall, Texas. He attended the University of Texas in Austin from 1952 to 1956. Then he served for two years in the United States Army.

Upon his release from the military, he began a career in journalism as a reporter for the *Marshall News-Messenger* in Texas. Two years later he moved to the *Dallas News*, where he worked as a reporter until the *Philadelphia Inquirer* offered him a position in 1961.

Perhaps one of the most revered if not prolific investigative journalists who ever wrote an expose article or book, Goulden remained with the *Inquirer* until he resigned in 1968 to work as a freelance writer.

Goulden's *The Curtis Caper*, which was his first book, was published in 1965. This book was followed by other investigative reports, including *Monopoly*, which was published in 1968. In this book Goulden examined one of the most powerful and gigantic corporations on Earth—the American Telephone and Telegraph Company. *Truth Is the First Casualty: The Gulf of Tonkin Affair, Illusion and Reality* was published a year later and examined the complex Gulf of Tonkin incidents that were responsible for the United States expanding its involvement in Vietnam. *The Money Givers* was published in 1971. *Meany: The Unchallenged Strong Man of American Labor* was published in 1972 and painted a different portrait of one of America's labor bosses. *The Superlawyers: The Small and Powerful World of the Great Washington Law Firms* was published the same year. In traditional muckraking fashion, Goulden disclosed the corruption of certain Washington law firms and the collusion between their employees and members of the federal government. *The Benchwarmers: The Small and Powerful World of the Great Federal Judges* was published in 1974 and disrobed the judges for their unlawful decisions. *The Million Dollar Lawyers* was published in 1978 and examined the questionable conduct of the most expensive legal representatives. *Korea: The Untold Story of the War* was published in 1982 and presented an accurate history of the Korean War. *Jerry Wurf: Labor's Last Angry Man* was published in 1982.

Goulden received praise from numerous reviewers for several of his in-depth studies, particularly *Monopoly*, *Truth Is the First Casualty*, *The Superlawyers*, and *The Benchwarmers*.

With Paul Dickson, Goulden co-wrote *There Are Alligators in Our Sewers, and Other American Credos*, which was published in 1983. To say the least, this book's subject matter was a change of pace.

In addition to the books mentioned above, Goulden contributed incisive exposes to such periodicals as the *Texas Observer*, *Texas Monthly*, *Harper's Magazine*, and *The Nation*.

In 1984, with Alexander W. Raffio, he co-wrote *The Death Merchant: The Rise and Fall of Edwin P. Wilson*. The book concerned the one-time intelligence officer who had worked for the Central Intelligence Agency (CIA) until his contract was not renewed in 1971. Wilson had betrayed his country by agreeing to provide explosives and personnel to Colonel Muammar el-Qaddafi. Fortunately, others learned about Wilson's plan before it was executed. The book penetrated the intelligence community and explained how it operated.

Four years later Goulden wrote *Fit to Print: A. M. Rosenthal and His Times*, which concerned the editor of *The New York Times*. Filled with anecdotal material, the gossipy biography was written primarily to titillate the reader, not necessarily to provide a well-balanced profile of the subject.

Although Goulden became a media critic for Accuracy in Media, Inc., in 1989, he continued to research and write books. For instance, in 1993, with Reed Irvine and Cliff Kincaid, he co-wrote *The News Manipulators: Why You Can't Trust the News*, which told about the news industry and how it does not necessarily disseminate information based on facts.

In 2006 he wrote *The Money Lawyers: the No-holds Barred World of Today's Richest and Most Powerful Lawyers*, which examined some of the most powerful law firms in the United States.

Goulden employed a direct approach in his books. Seldom did he use excess words or sentences. He presented the facts and his observations based on those facts. Goulden exposed his subjects by providing incidents or examples.

Like other investigative journalists, he informed the American people of wrong-doing. His book *Monopoly* undoubtedly influenced politicians to examine the American Telephone and Telegraph Company and its hold on the communications industry. Eventually, this examination led to the company's breakup. Goulden's book *Truth Is the First Casualty: The Gulf of Tonkin Affair, Illusion and Reality* opened the eyes and minds of readers, including politicians, to the fact that the Gulf of Tonkin affair may not have happened as it had been reported. His other exposes had similar effects.

Representative Works

The Curtis Caper, 1965.
Monopoly, 1968.
Truth Is the First Casualty: The Gulf of Tonkin Affair, Illusion and Reality, 1969.
The Money Givers, 1971.
Meany: The Unchallenged Strong Man of American Labor, 1972.
The Superlawyers: The Small and Powerful World the Great Washington Law Firms, 1972.
The Benchwarmers: The Small and Powerful World of the Great Federal Judges, 1974.
The Million Dollar Lawyers, 1978.
Korea: The Untold Story of the War, 1982.
Jerry Wurf: Labor's Last Angry Man, 1982.
The Death Merchant: The Rise and Fall of Edwin P. Wilson (with Alexander W. Raffio), 1984.
Fit to Print: A. M. Rosenthal and His Times, 1985.

Further Reading

Alfisi, Kathryn. "A Conversation with Joseph Goulden." *The Washington Lawyer* 20.10 (June 2006).

Goulden, Joseph C. *Contemporary Authors*. Vols. 17–20, 1st Rev. Detroit: Gale Research, 1976.

Goulden, Joseph C. *Contemporary Authors, New Revision Series*. Vol. 31. Detroit: Gale Research, 1990.

Goulden, Joseph C. "No Investigative Reporting." *American Journalism Review* 15 (Sept. 1993).

Robert W. Greene (1929–2008)

Investigative journalist Robert W. Greene was born in Queens on July 12, 1929, and attended Fordham University in the late 1940s.

In 1949 he worked as a reporter for the *Jersey Journal*, a position he held until he was offered an investigative position with the New York City Anti-crime Commission a year later.

He moved to *Newsday*, a tabloid-sized Long Island newspaper, in 1955. First, he worked as a reporter. Then, from 1967 to 1973, he served as the leader of the investigative team. He became a senior editor in 1970 and an assistant managing editor in 1974.

Together with other writers at *Newsday*, Greene co-wrote the phenomenally best-selling novel *Naked Came the Stranger* in 1970.

His work as an investigative journalist gained attention. For instance, when the team was initiated in 1967, its first target was the unorthodox zoning practices in Long Island townships. The team reported that developers had bribed local officials to rezone certain areas so developers could build on land they would not have been able to use otherwise. After two years of stories, at least seven persons were indicted and convicted, at least thirty public officials resigned from their positions, and new legislation was enacted.

In 1969 Greene and another reporter at *Newsday* retraced Ted Kennedy's footsteps in Chappaquidick and wrote an inquisitive story that raised several questions about Kennedy's actions after his car went off a bridge. Greene, who had written about the Kennedys earlier in his career, had been a friend of Robert F. Kennedy before Kennedy was assassinated. Needless to say, his relationship with the Kennedys was severed after this story was published.

Two years later the team reported on Richard Nixon's lifestyle, investments, and friends in Florida. The Nixon White House reacted by putting the newspaper and its reporters on the White House enemies list.

Perhaps the team's most ambitious investigative work concerned the heroin trail from Turkey to New York City, which took months to unravel and present to the public because the team lived in Turkey, France, Mexico, and in several cities in the United States. The series was worth the time and expense, however, because it won a Pulitzer Prize in 1974; more important, it set a goal for other newspapers to try to achieve.

When *Arizona Republic* reporter Don Bolles was killed by a car bomb, Greene headed a team of reporters and editors from around the nation who investigated what Bolles had been researching. The team worked tirelessly for five months and uncovered a link between organized crime and political corruption, land fraud, and illegal drugs in Arizona. The stories were carried by the Associated Press (AP) and appeared in various newspapers around the country.

According to Steven J. Stark, the series of articles "was a hallmark event in journalism—one of the most ambitious stories ever done. It became known as the Arizona Project—and Bob Greene became a legend."[1]

Greene's investigative work was seen again in 1981 in *The Sting Man: Inside ABSCAM*, a book which explained the Federal Bureau of Investigation's (FBI) operation in detail and presented quite candidly Greene's assessment of Melvin R. Weinberg, the principal participant.

Throughout the 1980s, primarily because of his position at the Suffolk County bureau, Greene influenced numerous reporters and editors who worked at *Newsday*. Although he was demanding, he made certain that his team of reporters covered the lighter sides of life. He even had reporters write about Halloween by having them dress in costumes and go trick-or-treating. He was also instrumental in hiring female reporters out of college and teaching them the fundamentals of investigating and reporting hard news.

Greene retired from *Newsday* in 1992. He contributed an occasional op-ed column to the newspaper, however, and became an adjunct professor of journalism at Hofstra University as well as the State University of New York at Stony Brook.

He died April 10, 2008.

Representative Works

Newsday (Senior Editor, Assistant Managing Editor).
The Sting Man: Inside ABSCAM, 1981.

Further Reading

Greene, Robert W. *Contemporary Authors*. Vol. 104. Detroit: Gale Research, 1982.
Greene, Robert W. *Contemporary Authors*. Vol. 271. Detroit: Gale, Cengage Learning, 2008.
Marro, Anthony. "Role Model: A Larger-than-Life Reporter: Bob Greene Taught Newsday Journalists How to Investigate Corruption with a Flourish." *Columbia Journalism Review* 40.6 (Mar.–Apr. 2002).
Robert W. Greene. "Journalist Was Pulitzer Winner." *Los Angeles Times* (3 Apr. 2008).
"Robert W. Greene". *Journalism & Mass Communication Educator* 64.3 (Autumn, 2009).
Stark, Steven J. "Investigating Bob Greene." *The Quill* 81.5 (June, 1993).

1 Steven J. Stark, "Investigating Bob Greene: His Mighty Ax Felled Presidential Timber and Cub Reporters Alike," *Quill* (June 1993), 17.

Leonard Gross (1928–2015)

Leonard Gross was born on April 21, 1928, in Chicago to Benjamin and Clara Gross. After graduating from high school, he attended the University of California at Los Angeles, from which he received his bachelor's degree in 1949. Then he attended Columbia University, from which he received his master's degree a year later.

Gross served in the United States Army before he entered the field of journalism as a reporter for *The Wall Street Journal*. Although he was assigned to the San Francisco bureau, he did not stay at the newspaper long. In 1952 he joined the staff of *The San Francisco Chronicle*, where he remained a few years.

In 1955 he traveled to New York City and joined the staff of *Collier's*. Although Gross enjoyed working as a journalist for newspapers and magazines, he worked as a freelance writer from 1956 to 1959, the year he was hired by the editors of *Look* magazine. Gross served as a senior editor in New York City, as a Latin American correspondent in Rio de Janeiro, as a European editor in Paris, and as a West Coast editor in Los Angeles. He remained with *Look* for several years, until it ceased publication in the 1970s.

Gross became a theater critic for *Westways* magazine in the early 1970s. He held this position until 1980. After he left the magazine, he spent his time as a freelance writer. His experiences, particularly those he had with *Look*, were incorporated into articles and books.

Gross wrote about politics, journalism, fitness, history, social drinking, and, with Raymond Dirks, unscrupulous business practices. *The Great Wall Street Scandal*, which was written with Dirks in 1974, explained Dirks's role in the downfall of the Equity Funding Corporation (see the entry on Dirks elsewhere in this book for additional information).

In 1982 Gross wrote *The Last Jews in Berlin*. This book, which was based on numerous interviews with Jewish survivors who had hid in Berlin during World War II, presented an emotional portrait of a courageous group of people who had been despised by the Nazis but had escaped the Nazi death camps.

Gross co-wrote *The Dossier* with Pierre Salinger in 1984. Other novels as well as a few works of nonfiction followed.

In 2013 his novel *The Memoirs of JFK: If Kennedy Had Survived* was published. Based on interviews with numerous individuals who had known the president or had covered his years in office, the novel focused on the president surviving the assassination attempt in Dallas, his two terms as president, and the memoir he wrote after leaving the presidency.

Gross died April 23, 2015.

Representative Works

The Great Wall Street Scandal (with Raymond Dirks), 1974.
The Last Jews in Berlin, 1982.

Further Reading

Gross, Leonard. *Contemporary Authors*. Vol. 112. Detroit: Gale Research, 1985.
Gross, Leonard. *Contemporary Authors*. Vol. 118. Detroit: Gale Research, 1986.

Richard Harris (1928–1987)

Richard Harris reportedly was born in 1928, although this year is not definitive. He was an investigative reporter for *The New Yorker* before he started writing novels in the late 1970s.

After he had written about politics in America for the magazine for nine years, he wrote his first book-length expose in 1964. In *The Real Voice*, Harris analyzed Senator Estes Kefauver's investigation into the drug industry's unscrupulous practices of selling and overpricing products. In *A Sacred Trust*, which was published two years later, he vehemently attacked the American Medical Association for its uncaring politics concerning medical care for the aged. In 1969 he expanded the article "The Turning Point," which had appeared in *The New Yorker*, into the informative, fully documented book, *Fear of Crime*. Basically a critique of the Omnibus Crime Bill of 1968, which had been passed by President Lyndon Johnson in response to the fear of crime and not to an increase in criminal acts, Harris claimed the bill, because of its nature, overturned the United States Supreme Court's decisions in the Wade, Mallory, and Miranda cases. In fact, the bill allowed authorities to wire-tap anyone who was considered to be a threat to national security or connected to organized crime for forty-eight hours without having to go to a judge.

Harris wrote *Justice: The Crisis of Law, Order and Freedom in America* a year later. Harris analyzed the operations of the Justice Department under Ramsey Clark and later John Mitchell. Although Harris admired Clark's refusal to politicize the Justice Department, he was severely critical of Mitchell and President Richard Nixon when they approved funds to be used arbitrarily by police departments. Harris also criticized the politicization of the Justice Department by Mitchell as well as his failure to stop illogical and immoral acts performed by various police departments across the country.

In 1971 Harris wrote the scathing book *Decision*, a detailed, analytical account of President Nixon and John Mitchell's attempt to put an apparent racist, G. Harrold Carswell, on the United States Supreme Court. Harris noted:

> Of all the actions that President Richard Nixon took during his first two years in office, probably none more clearly revealed the character of his Presidency—the regional and class appeals that divided the nation, the disregard for the Constitutional separation of powers, the embittered relations between the Administration and the Senate, the apparent confidence that the people would sleep through even the noisiest raid on their liberties, and the belief that members of Congress could be counted on to

> put their own political interest above the public interest—than his nomination of George Harrold Carswell, of Florida, to be an associate justice of the Supreme Court.[1]

Harris revealed the political shenanigans that were deployed by the administration. Fortunately, Senator Birch Bayh of Indiana and others learned about Carswell's discriminatory record and persuaded loyal Nixon supporters to resist the pressures from the White House. Carswell was defeated, and Nixon never recovered.

Five years later Harris examined three cases in which people's civil rights had been grossly overlooked by representative bodies of the federal government. He claimed the federal government was unaware of people's needs and the judiciary served the state in most cases. He advocated that any representative body should adhere to the Constitution. If it failed to do so, then it should have to pay the consequences.

In August 1987, Harris fell from his apartment window and died. The authorities ruled that he had committed suicide.

Representative Works

The Real Voice, 1964.
A Sacred Trust, 1966.
Fear of Crime, 1969.
Justice: The Crisis of Law, Order and Freedom in America, 1970.
Decision, 1971.

Further Reading

Harris, Richard. *Contemporary Authors*, Vol. 123. Detroit: Gale Research, 1988.
Harris, Richard. *Contemporary Authors*, Vol. 129. Detroit: Gale Research, 1990.
"Obituary." *The New York Times Biographical Service* 18 (Aug. 1987).
Harris, Richard. *New Yorker* 63.31 (21 Sept. 1987).

1 Richard Harris, *Decision* (New York: E. P. Dutton, 1971), 10.

Diana B. Henriques (1948–)

Investigative business and financial journalist Diana Henriques was born in late 1948 in Bryan, Texas, but grew up in Roanoke, Virginia. She became interested in journalism when she experienced it at *The Roanoke Times and World News* in Virginia. She was in her teens.

Henriques worked on her high school newspaper before she graduated in 1966. She earned a scholarship and attended George Washington University, where she enrolled in courses in the School of Public and International Affairs (now The Elliott School of International Affairs) and worked on *The Hatchet*, the student newspaper, before she graduated in 1969.

She married Laurence B. Henriques, Jr., the same year, and worked at several newspapers in New Jersey. For instance, she worked as an editor at *The Lawrence Ledger*, a small paper in Lawrence Township, and as a government reporter at the *Asbury Park Press*, a small paper in Asbury Park.

Henriques also gained journalism experience when she worked for *The Times* in Trenton, New Jersey. In fact, primarily because of an assignment, she had to learn about the municipal bond market and other financial subjects. As a result of her informal education, she wrote articles about these topics as well as about the housing authority.

When she worked for *The Philadelphia Inquirer*, she wrote more stories about business and financial subjects, including Wall Street. In 1986 she joined the staff of *Barron's* magazine, for which she wrote news stories and feature articles. *The Machinery of Greed: Public Authority Abuse and What to Do about It*, her first book, was published the same year and concerned governmental agencies that were responsible for millions of dollars but often had inexperienced or corrupt individuals or firms overseeing the funds. Needless to say, the book contained actual incidents of such agencies losing money because of little or no oversight.

Henriques moved to *The New York Times* three years later. She wrote articles about business and finance, including Wall Street.

She wrote the book *Fidelity's World: The Secret Life and Public Power of the Mutual Fund Giant*, which was published in 1995. The book concerned one of the largest stock-trading operations in the world. Fidelity has billions and billions of dollars in mutual funds, corporate retirement plans, and private partnerships. The book examined the company's history and operation.

She wrote a series in 1996 that explained how wealthy Americans were not paying their fair share of taxes primarily because of tax breaks provided to them by Congress and the laws the body wrote.

In 1997 Henriques suffered an injury that forced her to use a voice-recognition software program for whatever she wrote, no matter whether it was an article or book. Still, she was productive. For instance, she revealed the near-collapse of Long Term Capital Management, a hedge-fund company. She, along with a few others who worked with her, received a Gerald Loeb Award in 1999.

The White Sharks of Wall Street: Thomas Mellon Evans and the Original Corporate Raiders was published in 2000 and concerned the mavericks and corporate raiders who appeared after World War II, including Thomas Mellon Evans, who eventually controlled more than eighty American companies. Evans was a champion for shareholders before it was fashionable to do so. He was responsible for companies getting rid of departments or areas that were not necessary in order to increase profits. Of course, other individuals were discussed in the book as well.

In 2001 she and another writer at the newspaper investigated various problems in the country's scholastic testing industry. The same year she and David Barstow examined the federal program that was established primarily to compensate survivors of those killed in the attacks on September 11, 2001.

She wrote about Cantor Fitzgerald, a trading company that lost most of its employees when the World Trade Center collapsed.

Henriques was elected to the Board of Governors of the Society of American Business Editors and Writers in 2003.

A year later she wrote "Captive Clientele," a series about how insurance companies and financial firms, particularly those on or near military bases that were managed by former military officers, were selling unsuitable policies and other products to military soldiers who did not necessarily understand what they were buying or why. For this series, Henriques conducted every interview and examined every relevant document she could find. As a result of her series, she earned a few journalism awards or prizes, and state and federal legislation was ultimately enacted primarily to protect military personnel from such companies.

In 2011 *The Wizard of Lies: Bernie Madoff and the Death of Trust* was published. The book was based on her work about Madoff who had founded a large brokerage firm and who had confessed to operating the largest Ponzi scheme at the time in the nation's history. Of course, Madoff had earned money, but his investors had not. The same year *The New York Times* printed an interview Henriques had with Madoff, who was serving time in prison for his crimes. The book became the basis for a film in 2017.

A year later, instead of serving as an investigative journalist for the newspaper, Henriques negotiated a contract that allowed her to become a contributing writer instead. The same year she received the Distinguished Achievement Award from the Society for Advancing Business and Editing and Writing.

For 2012–2013, she received a Ferris professorship in writing at Princeton University.

In 2017 *A First-Class Catastrophe: The Road to Black Monday, the Worst Day in Wall Street History* was published. The book concerned "Black Monday," which was October 19, 1987, and was one of the worst days on Wall Street. Indeed, the stock market crashed almost twenty-three percent, or 508 points. Henriques presented the history leading up to and after the crash. She interviewed numerous individuals for the book. Without question, the book revealed the causes for the crash.

Representative Works

"Captive Clientele," 2004.
Fidelity's World: The Secret Life and Public Power of the Mutual Fund Giant, 1995.
A First-Class Catastrophe: The Road to Black Monday, the Worst Day in Wall Street History, 2017.
The Machinery of Greed: Public Authority Abuse and What to Do about It, 1986.
"Those Who Don't Learn From Financial Crises Are Doomed to Repeat Them," 2017.
The White Sharks of Wall Street: Thomas Mellon Evans and the Original Corporate Raiders, 2000.
The Wizard of Lies: Bernie Madoff and the Death of Trust, 2011.

Further Reading

Bedway, Barbara. "How the Paper Chase Earns Awards." *Editor & Publisher* 138.5 (May 2005). (www.dianabhenriques.com).

Seymour Hersh (1937–)

Born in Chicago on April 8, 1937, Seymour Hersh graduated from the University of Chicago in 1958.

Hersh began his reporting career in 1959 as a police reporter for the Chicago City News Bureau. Within three years he moved to the United Press International (UPI), for which he worked as a correspondent. In 1963 he obtained a position with the Associated Press (AP) and served as a correspondent in Chicago and Washington, D.C. Aggressive, brash, and eager to get a story, Hersh covered the Pentagon. However, he refused to accept press announcements from officials. Instead, he roamed the building's corridors to find military brass and systems analysis personnel who had access to the truth. Ultimately, he learned about chemical and biological warfare research. Hersh realized the information was sensational. He wrote several articles based on the information, but the AP refused them.

Disagreeing with the editors' policies, Hersh quit his job and submitted the articles to periodicals, which accepted them. The articles described the development of chemical and biological warfare agents and identified the corporations and universities that produced them for the government. Hersh even mentioned where these warfare agents were stored. Later, the articles were included in the book *Chemical and Biological Warfare: America's Hidden Arsenal*, which was published in 1968.

When Senator Eugene McCarthy campaigned for president in 1968, Hersh worked for him as a press secretary until the Wisconsin primary, but politics was not for him. He returned to Washington and contributed articles to *The New Republic*, *The Progressive*, *Ramparts*, and other magazines.

In 1969 Hersh investigated the My Lai massacre, which the AP had disclosed. Although he was advised by various members of the United States Army as well as the federal government not to write about the incident, Hersh traveled across the United States to interview Lieutenant William Calley, who, according to army officials, had ordered the killing of 109 Vietnamese civilians. Hersh gave the story to the Dispatch News Service to sell to newspapers. He immediately followed up this story with another story concerning the men under Calley's command. Eventually, Hersh wrote about one veteran who had participated in the My Lai Four massacre. The veteran, who was ashamed of what he had been ordered to do, appeared on the "CBS Evening News" and informed viewers of the atrocity. Hersh continued the series for the Dispatch News Service and wrote the book *My Lai Four: A Report on the Massacre and Its Aftermath*, which was published in 1970. The book was based on information provided by witnesses and depicted graphically what had occurred.

Hersh won a Pulitzer Prize for his stories. He investigated other atrocities related to the Vietnam War. For instance, he disclosed the apparent cover-up of My Lai and similar incidents by the army. He revealed that lower-ranking officers had become scapegoats for carrying out orders that had been given by higher-ranking officers. The reports were published in *The New Yorker* and then in *Cover-Up: The Army's Secret Investigation of the Massacre of My Lai Four*, which was published in 1972.

The same year Hersh joined the Washington bureau of *The New York Times*. He wrote about the secret bombing of North Vietnam and Cambodia. He also disclosed several important facts about Watergate. For instance, he revealed the burglars, although apprehended, were receiving money on a regular basis. In another story, he presented the persons responsible for the burglars' monetary support. Hersh also disclosed that President Richard Nixon, in order to learn who was leaking information concerning Watergate, authorized Henry Kissinger to have telephones wiretapped. In other stories, Hersh informed readers about President Nixon's secret war in Cambodia; agents from the Pentagon had stolen secret documents from Kissinger's office; Air Force General John D. Lavelle had ordered unauthorized bombings of North Vietnam; the CIA had attempted to raise a sunken Soviet submarine in the Pacific; the CIA had spied on certain private citizens in the United States; and the CIA had attempted to overthrow President Salvador Allende of Chile.

In the mid-1970s Hersh moved to the newspaper's New York City offices, where he continued his investigative reporting. He left the paper in 1979, however, to write books.

In 1983 Hersh became a contributing editor to *The Atlantic Monthly*. The same year his book *The Price of Power: Kissinger in the Nixon White House* was published. The book had taken almost four years to write because of the hundreds of interviews he had conducted. A critical expose, the book revealed Kissinger's calculated machinations, including his straddling the political fence in 1968. According to Hersh, Kissinger fed secret information about the Paris peace talks to members of the Nixon campaign. Concurrently, Kissinger offered Nelson Rockefeller's files about Nixon to members of Humphrey's campaign. These actions were supposedly taken so he would have a position in the administration no matter who won the presidential election. Hersh also explained that Kissinger and Nixon had agreed on the overriding principle that guided the policies in Vietnam: South Vietnam had to remain non-Communist, no matter what. Secret massive bombings occurred in Cambodia primarily because of this principle. Of course, Hersh examined Kissinger and Nixon's so-called successes, such as the SALT Treaty with the former Soviet Union, with a critical eye and a sarcastic tone. Although numerous reviewers praised the book for its insight, several critics claimed that many of those interviewed had been dismissed from their jobs or had been forced to resign. Nonetheless, the book earned Hersh a National Book Critics Circle Award in general nonfiction a year later.

"The Target Is Destroyed": What Really Happened to Flight 007 and What America Knew About It was published in 1987. From countless interviews, Hersh recounted the events and claimed the passenger plane had merely flown off course unintentionally and the former Soviet Union had responded in haste. The book was packed with anecdotal material and revealed how officials in Washington, D.C., and Moscow interpreted the fragmentary data in terms of their own world view.

The Samson Option: Israel, America and the Bomb was published in 1991. In this book Hersh explored a topic that had been discussed by members of the media for several years. Hersh exposed the top-secret Israeli nuclear-weapons program, describing how the Israelis had procured the bomb, how the American government had helped its ally, and why the Israelis had not actually needed America's help. The book presented the whole story—from the 1920s to the war with Iraq. Hersh claimed he knew how many bombs were in Israel as well as where they were stored. However, several of his claims were undocumented. Nonetheless, the book was intriguing and illustrated Hersh's skills as an investigative journalist.

The Dark Side of Camelot was published in 1997 and focused on President John F. Kennedy. Hersh made several assertions about the president that were considered controversial by reviewers. For instance, he claimed the president had been prescribed an amphetamine-related drug and had a working relationship with a well-known Mafia figure, among others. Critics claimed Hersh had relied on unsubstantiated hearsay evidence, not facts.

A year later *Against All Enemies: Gulf War Syndrome: The War Between America's Ailing Veterans and Their Government* was published. In this book Hersh exposed the problems Gulf War veterans had with the Veterans Administration and its hospitals.

In 2004 *Chain of Command: The Road from 9/11 to Abu Ghraib* was published. This book was based on Hersh's articles about the war in Iraq that had appeared in *The New Yorker*. Hersh exposed the so-called abuse of inmates at Abu Ghraib prison.

Hersh criticized President Barack Obama's administration in *The Killing of Osama Bin Ladin*, which was published in 2016.

Two years later Hersh's autobiography, *Reporter: A Memoir*, was published. Reviewers appreciated his comments about the need for investigative journalism as well as his comments about the state of journalism in general.

Representative Works

Chemical and Biological Warfare: America's Hidden Arsenal, 1968.
My Lai Four: A Report on the Massacre and Its Aftermath, 1970.
Cover-Up: The Army's Secret Investigation of the Massacre of My Lai Four, 1972.
The Price of Power: Kissinger in the Nixon White House, 1983.
"The Target Is Destroyed": What Really Happened to Flight 007 and What America Knew About It, 1987.
The Samson Option: Israel, America and the Bomb, 1991.
The Dark Side of Camelot, 1997.
Against All Enemies: Gulf War Syndrome: The War Between America's Ailing Veterans and Their Government, 1998.
Chain of Command: The Road from 9/11 to Abu Ghraib, 2004.
The Killing of Osama Bin Ladin, 2016.

Further Reading

Hersh, Seymour M. *Reporter: A Memoir*. New York: Alfred A. Knopf, 2018.
Isaac, Rael Jean. "Investigating Seymour Hersh." *Society* 43.1 (Nov.–Dec. 2005).
Kirchick, James. "The Deceits of Seymour Hersh: Chronicling a Singular Career in Meretricious Journalism." *Commentary* 133.3 (Mar. 2012).
Massing, Michael. "Breaking News: Seymour Hersh and the Ambiguities of Investigative Reporting." *Nation* 307.9 (22 Oct. 2018).
Miraldi, Robert. *Seymour Hersh: Scoop Artist*. Lincoln: Potomac Books, an imprint of the University of Nebraska Press, 2013.
Rosen, James. "Scoop." *National Interest* 157 (Sept.–Oct. 2018)
Seymour Hersh. *Current Biography Yearbook*. 1984 ed. New York: H. W. Wilson Co., 1985.

Warren Hinckle (1938–2016)

Born in San Francisco in 1938, Warren Hinckle attended the University of San Francisco, where he served as the editor of the university newspaper. He left the university without a degree in 1960. He worked in public relations before he began his professional career in journalism at the *San Francisco Chronicle*. Hired as a reporter, Hinckle was assigned the police beat.

In 1964 he became the editor of *Ramparts*. Without question, his best efforts at investigative reporting occurred while serving as editor of this magazine, which had been founded two years earlier primarily as a forum for members of the Catholic Church. However, under Hinckle's guidance the magazine's direction changed. Instead of publishing articles that discussed certain trends in Catholicism, Hinckle published investigative articles about various major issues, including the atrocities in Vietnam that had been committed by personnel of the United States Army as well as the CIA's involvement in so-called independent organizations. Needless to say, such articles aroused readers' interests. As a result, the magazine's circulation increased from 3,000 to 300,000.

Unfortunately, Hinckle's high living eventually forced the magazine into the red. He left in 1969, and, with his friend, Sidney Zion, co-founded *Scanlan's Monthly*, a magazine that was similar to *Ramparts* in the sense that it published investigative articles, too. In fact, the magazine published Hunter S. Thompson's "The Kentucky Derby Is Decadent and Depraved," the first example of Thompson's so-called gonzo journalism. However, *Scanlan's Monthly* had a short life

In 1971 Hinckle's first book, *Guerrilla Warfare in the USA*, was published. In his untiring style, Hinckle discussed the numerous underground activities that had occurred across the United States. His best-known book, however, was *If You Have a Lemon, Make Lemonade: An Essential Memoir of a Lunatic Decade*, which was published in 1974. The book was a collection of articles, including the controversial essay about the investigation of the Kennedy assassination by James Garrison that had been published in *Ramparts*.

Hinckle contributed articles to various periodicals, including *Playboy*, *The Nation*, *The Atlantic Monthly*, and *Esquire*. He edited the magazine *City of San Francisco* in the mid-1970s, before he became a columnist for the *San Francisco Chronicle* in 1977.

In 1980 he collaborated with William Turner on the book *The Fish Is Red: The Story of the Secret War Against Castro*, which exposed the secret war against Fidel Castro and his Cuban regime. The book discussed the CIA's useless, sometimes senseless, military as well as civilian efforts, including its unsettling, if not frightening, relationship with certain criminal factions. The book was characteristic of Hinckle's arresting style.

In 1986 Hinckle was lured away from the *San Francisco Chronicle* by the publisher of the *San Francisco Examiner*. He worked as an associate editor and wrote a column about San Francisco.

Several years later he wrote a column for the *San Francisco Independent*, which had been founded in 1987. Hinckle's column concerned his political beliefs, among other subjects.

In 1993 he revived *The Argonaut*, a periodical that lasted several years. The same year *Deadly Secrets: The CIA-Mafia War Against Castro and the Assassination of JFK*, a book he had written with William Turner several years before, was updated and reprinted. Hinckle and Turner contended that a mélange of anti-Castro Cubans, Mafiosi, anti-communists, and operatives of the CIA played a major role in the Bay of Pigs invasion, the assassination of John F. Kennedy, Watergate, and the Iran-Contra scandal, among other incidents. The authors claimed that George Bush, the former director of the CIA, was connected to drug traffickers in Latin America as well as to the murderers of Orlando Letetier. As several reviewers noted, the book was riddled with holes. Consequently, it lacked credibility.

Hinckle died of pneumonia August 25, 2016, in San Francisco.

The book *Ransoming Pagan Babies: The Selected Writings of Warren Hinckle* was published two years later.

Representative Works

Ramparts (Editor).
Scanlan's Monthly (Co-founder and Editor).
Guerrilla Warfare in the USA, 1971.
The Fish Is Red: The Story of the Secret War Against Castro (with William Turner), 1980.
Deadly Secrets: The CIA-Mafia War Against Castro and the Assassination of JFK (with William Turner), reprinted 1993.

Further Reading

Black, Pam. "The Classic: *Ramparts* (1962–1975): Bringing the New Left to Middle America." *Folio: The Magazine for Magazine Management* 3.4 (Apr. 2004).
Collier, Peter. "The Passing of a Sixties Showman." *New Criterion* 35.2 (Oct. 2016)

Grimes, William. "Warren Hinckle, Editor of Ramparts and Voice for Radical Left, Dies At 77." *The New York Times* (26 Aug. 2016).

Hinckle, Warren. *Contemporary Authors*. Vols. 89–92. Detroit: Gale Research, 1980.

Richardson, Peter. *A Bomb in Every Issue: How the Short, Unruly Life of Ramparts Magazine Changed America*. New York: New Press, 2009.

Smith, Harrison. "Warren Hinckle, Editor of the Swaggering 60s Magazine Ramparts, Dies at 77." *The Washington Post* (30 Aug. 2016).

Ronald Kessler (1943–)

Ronald Kessler was born on December 31, 1943, to Minuetta and Ernest Borek, in New York, New York. His mother and father later divorced. When his mother remarried, Kessler adopted his step-father's last name.

Kessler attended Clark University for two years, from 1962 to 1964, before he became a journalist for *The Worcester Telegram* in Worcester, Massachusetts. Soon, he got a job as an investigative journalist and editorial writer with *The Boston Herald*.

In 1968 he moved to *The Wall Street Journal* in New York City, where he stayed until he moved to *The Washington Post* in 1970. Kessler worked as an investigative journalist for the *Post* for fifteen years. He received several awards for his journalism over the years. For instance, in 1965 he received the Sevellon Brown Award from the Associated Press (AP). In 1972 he received a George Polk Award for his series about the mismanagement of non-profit hospitals as well as his series about questionable or illegal fees charged to homebuyers. In 1978 he received a George Polk Award for his articles about corruption in the General Services Administration (GSA).

The Life Insurance Game, Kessler's first book, was published in 1985. Kessler penetrated the life insurance business, specifically, its questionable sales tactics which were employed to appeal to new subscribers. He also pointed out that the industry was not overseen by the federal government.

The Richest Man in the World: The Story of Adnan Khashoggi was published in 1986. Kessler provided a glance into the life of the Middle Easterner who started out with very little only to end up with a fortune before his death. Khashoggi provided arms and other merchandise to the royal family in Saudi Arabia.

In 1987 *Spy vs. Spy: Stalking Soviet Spies in America* was published. For this book Kessler interviewed counterintelligence agents of the Federal Bureau of Investigation (FBI) and reported about their successful operations. He also interviewed several spies who had been apprehended and convicted of spying on the United States. Kessler revealed how the United States and the Soviet Union employed spies to learn about their so-called enemies.

Moscow Station: How the KGB Penetrated the American Embassy was published in 1989. Kessler covered the breach caused by several individuals, including a few Marines as well as others, who worked at the American Embassy in Moscow. In essence, it was rather easy for the Russians to gather information at the embassy because of carelessness by those employed there. In fact, many would say these people were reckless.

A year later *The Spy in the Russian Club: How Glenn Souther Stole American Nuclear War Plans and Escaped to Moscow* was published. Kessler presented Glenn Souther, including his experiences in the United States Navy, and claimed Souther had access to certain critical information before he ended up in Russia. The question is was Souther working for the Russians?

In 1991 *Escape from the CIA: How the CIA Won and Lost the Most Important KGB Spy Ever to Defect to the U. S.* was published. In this book Kessler provided a detailed account of Vitaly Yurchenko, a colonel who supposedly defected to the United States and informed his U. S. handlers about the KGB. Then Yurchenko returned to the Soviet Union. Like Kessler's previous books, this book was well documented.

Inside the CIA: Revealing the Secrets of the World's Most Powerful Spy Agency was published a year later. Kessler examined the structure of the Central Intelligence Agency (CIA). Indeed, he divulged how the agency operated, from the director on down.

In 1993 *The FBI: Inside the World's Most Powerful Law Enforcement Agency* was published. In this book Kessler discussed the workings of the FBI, including its operation to uncover spies in the United States.

Inside the White House: The Hidden Lives of the Modern President and the Secrets of the World's Most Powerful Institution was published in 1995. Kessler revealed the lives of several first families who occupied the White House, and how the Secret Service operated to protect the president and members of his family.

His in-depth biography of Joe Kennedy was published in 1996. Titled *The Sins of the Father: Joseph P. Kennedy and the Dynasty He Founded*, the book was based on interviews with individuals who had firsthand knowledge about certain aspects of Joe Kennedy's life.

A year later *Inside Congress: The Shocking Scandals, Corruption, and Abuse of Power behind the Scenes on Capitol Hill* was published. Based on interviews with individuals who worked inside the capitol, Kessler revealed more than what the average American reader suspected about his or her members of Congress and the Senate.

The Season: Inside Palm Beach and America's Richest Society was published in 1999. In this book Kessler presented various tales primarily through the steps of four residents about the island community. Needless to say, the book was a departure for the author who usually reported about the various institutions in Washington, D. C.

In 2002 *The Bureau: The Secret History of the FBI* was published. Kessler presented the history of the organization, from its founding in 1908 to 2002, including the reasons for it not being prepared for the attacks on September 11, 2001.

The CIA at War: Inside the Secret Campaign against Terror was published in 2003. For this book Kessler had access to the director and numerous officers. Kessler explained how the director had pointed the agency in a different direction. Indeed, employees had to understand terrorism, learn who the terrorists were, and then hunt the terrorists down. In addition to presenting the agency's successes, Kessler presented its failures, too.

A Matter of Character: Inside the White House of George W. Bush was published in 2004. For this book Kessler interviewed numerous individuals and presented a portrait of the president that had not been revealed by the mainstream media. In fact, he presented a president who made decisions based on his moral compass, not on what other people thought.

In 2006 Kessler revealed Laura Bush in the appropriately titled book, *Laura Bush: An Intimate Portrait of the First Lady*. For this book Kessler interviewed numerous individuals who worked in the White House as well as personal friends of the First Lady. The biography captured the personality and character of Mrs. Bush.

The Terrorist Watch: Inside the Desperate Race to Stop the Next Attack was published in 2007. For this book Kessler interviewed directors and other officials in Washington, D. C., and elsewhere and explained how the country had escaped another terrorist attack as well as how its various institutions had helped other countries.

Two years later *In the President's Secret Service* was published. Kessler interviewed numerous current and former agents of the Secret Service and revealed previously untold stories about the various occupants of the White House. He also informed readers about the everyday operations of the Secret Service.

In 2011 *The Secrets of the FBI* was published. Kessler revealed the operation that led to Osama bin Laden's death. He explained Marilyn Monroe's death and Vince Foster's suicide. He told how the FBI caught Robert Hanssen, an agent who had sold information to the Russians.

Similar to the book *In the President's Secret Service*, Kessler's next book, *The First Family Detail: Secret Service Agents Reveal the Hidden Lives of the Presidents*, was published in 2014. Kessler presented several shocking revelations about the occupants of the White House, not to mention the sexual exploits of secret service agents.

In 2018 *The Trump White House: Changing the Rules of the Game* was published. For this book Kessler interviewed the president and others in the White House and depicted a president few people knew primarily because of the mainstream media, which favors the Left. Indeed, the media had painted a different portrait for their viewers or readers.

From 2006 to 2012 Kessler worked as a Washington correspondent for *Newsmax*. In addition to working for various publications and writing books, he contributed opinion pieces to several major newspapers and magazines.

Representative Works

The Life Insurance Game, 1985.
Spy vs. Spy: Stalking Soviet Spies in America, 1987.
Moscow Station: How the KGB Penetrated the American Embassy, 1989.
The Spy in the Russian Club: How Glenn Souther Stole America's Nuclear War Plans and Escaped to Moscow, 1990.
Inside the CIA: Revealing the Secrets of the World's Most Powerful Spy Agency, 1992.
The FBI: Inside the World's Most Powerful Law Enforcement Agency, 1993.
Inside the White House: The Hidden Lives of the Modern Presidents and the Secrets of the World's Most Powerful Institution, 1995.
Inside Congress: The Shocking Scandals, Corruption, and Abuse of Power behind the Scenes on Capitol Hill, 1997.
The Bureau: The Secret History of the FBI, 2002.
The CIA at War: Inside the Secret Campaign Against Terror, 2003.
The Terrorist Watch: Inside the Desperate Race to Stop the Next Attack, 2007.
In the President's Secret Service, 2009.
The Secrets of the FBI, 2011.
The First Family Detail: Secret Service Agents Reveal the Hidden Lives of the Presidents, 2014.

Further Reading

Kessler, Ronald. *Contemporary Authors: New Revision Series*. Volume 189. Detroit: Gale, Cengage Learning, 2009.
Kessler, Ronald. *Gale Literature: Contemporary Authors*. Detroit: Gale, Cengage Learning, 2011.
www.ronaldkessler.com.

Nick Kotz (1932–2020)

Nick Kotz was born to Jacob and Tybe Kotz on September 16, 1932, in San Antonio, Texas. He graduated from Dartmouth College in 1955 and then attended the London School of Economics.

He served as a lieutenant in the United States Marine Corps before he was hired as a reporter by the *Des Moines Register* in 1958. As a reporter, he learned how to obtain information important to his readers. For instance, he investigated the meat-packing industry and wrote a series of articles about the unsanitary conditions in several meat-packing plants. As a result, the series encouraged the passage of the Federal Wholesome Meat Act of 1967. Kotz received a Pulitzer Prize for the series in 1968.

He wrote the revealing and penetrating *Let Them Eat Promises: The Politics of Hunger in America*, which was published in 1969. According to Kotz,

> I first saw the realities of extreme rural poverty through the eyes of my wife, Mary Lynn, on a 1960 trip to her native state of Mississippi.... Working as a newspaper reporter, I saw similar suffering and injustice in Iowa, the golden breadbasket of this nation's prosperity. Returning to Mississippi and other parts of the rural South in 1967 as a Washington correspondent reporting on government programs supposedly designed to alleviate poverty, it seemed to me that the misery was worse than it had been seven years earlier.[1]

As several reviewers noted, Kotz had presented a disturbing piece of nonfiction. Indeed, he had discussed the problems, including the mismanagement by the federal government, the industrialization of the South, which had decreased the number of small farms, and the migration of African Americans from the South to the North.

Kotz contributed articles to various periodicals, including *The Progressive*, *Harper's Magazine*, *Look*, and *The Nation*.

In 1970 he joined the reporting staff of *The Washington Post*. Two years later he and Haynes Johnson, another *Post* reporter, wrote the articles that appeared under the title "The Unions." The articles surveyed historically the problems between labor, business, and government. The articles were revised and published as the book *The Unions* in 1972.

With his wife, Mary Lynn, Kotz wrote *A Passion for Equality: George A. Wiley and the Movement*, which was published in 1977. Eleven years later he

1 Nick Kotz, *Let Them Eat Promises: The Politics of Hunger in America* (Englewood Cliffs, N.J.: Prentice-Hall, 1969), xi.

wrote *Wild Blue Yonder: Money, Politics, and the B-1 Bomber*, which told the story of the failed attempts by the best engineers in the United States as well as Air Force strategists to design, produce, and deploy a state-of-the-art bomber. According to Kotz, the reason for these failed attempts was the political bureaucratic process of procurement, not engineering. Kotz examined three decades of military-industrial maneuvering—from President Eisenhower who said no to the concept to President Reagan who said yes.

Judgment Days: Lyndon Baines Johnson, Martin Luther King, Jr., and the Laws That Changed America was published in 2006. In this book Kotz examined the roles that President Johnson and Dr. Martin Luther King, Jr., played for civil rights legislation in the 1960s.

In 2013, in *The Harness Maker's Dream: Nathan Kallison and the Rise of South Texas*, Kotz candidly wrote about his grandfather, Nathan Kallison, who journeyed from the Ukraine to the United States in 1890. Kallison finally arrived in Chicago, where he learned to speak English and earn a living by making harnesses. Then he moved to San Antonio, Texas, where he ultimately started a successful farm and ranch supply business. The book undoubtedly was the most personal Kotz had written.

On April 26, 2020, Kotz died as a result of an unusual accident. He was hit by his own car when he tried to retrieve a package from the back seat.

Representative Works

Let Them Eat Promises: The Politics of Hunger in America, 1969.

Wild Blue Yonder: Money, Politics, and the B-1 Bomber, 1988.

Judgment Days: Lyndon Baines Johnson, Martin Luther King, Jr., and the Laws That Changed America, 2006.

Further Reading

Kotz, Nick. *Contemporary Authors*. Vols. 29–32, 1st Rev. Detroit: Gale Research, 1978.

Kotz, Nick. *Contemporary Authors, New Revision Series*. Vol. 162. Detroit: Gale, Cengage Learning, 2007.

Roberts, Sam. "Nick Kotz, 87, Who Won Pulitzer Prize for Exposing Hazards at Meat Plants." *The New York Times* (20 May 2020).

Schudel, Matt. "Nick Kotz, Author and Pulitzer Prize-Winning Journalist, Dies at 87." *The Washington Post* (28 Apr. 2020).

Jonathan Kwitny (1941–1998)

Born on March 23, 1941, to Julia and I. J. Kwitny, in Indianapolis, Indiana, Jonathan Kwitny majored in journalism at the University of Missouri, from which he graduated in 1962, and New York University, from which he earned his master's degree in 1964.

Kwitny worked as a reporter for *The News Tribune* in Perth Amboy, New Jersey, in the early 1960s. He took a leave from the newspaper to serve two years in the United States Peace Corps. In 1966 he returned to *The News Tribune*, where he remained until 1969, when he accepted a job as a reporter with *The New York Post* in New York City. From 1971 to 1988 he worked primarily as an investigative reporter for *The Wall Street Journal*.

In addition to his work for the latter newspaper, Kwitny wrote several books based on his investigations of various subjects, especially domestic and international corruption by American businesses, which had a tendency through lobbying organizations to influence individuals serving in the United States Congress to write and pass legislation that would help American businesses both stateside and abroad.

Kwitny interviewed numerous individuals in an effort to reveal the problems and issues about which he wrote.

His book *The Fountain Pen Conspiracy* was published in 1973 and exposed several so-called investment counselors who swindled clients out of their money. *The Mullendore Murder Case* followed in 1974. In this book Kwitny explored perhaps the biggest murder case in the history of Oklahoma. E. C. Mullendore, III, was 32 and lived at the Cross Bell Ranch in Osage County in northern Oklahoma. Wealthy but purportedly in debt, Mullendore supposedly had been insured for millions of dollars when he was murdered in 1970.

Along with Mullendore, Damon "Chub" Anderson, who worked for Mullendore, was shot in the shoulder. Anderson told the authorities he saw two young men in suits escape.

Kwitny explained what happened to Mullendore and provided financial details about him and the ranch. Although he implied who may have been involved, the case was never solved.

Vicious Circles: The Mafia in the Marketplace, which was published in 1979, brought Kwitny attention. In fact, Kwitny claimed the Mafia played a major role in American businesses, including food processing plants, banking and investment companies, and labor unions. As he had for his previous books, Kwitny did a lot of research for this one. In fact, this book was based on tape recordings with underworld figures, personal interviews, police reports, and trial transcripts. Kwitny documented how convicted Mafia officials were given light sentences primarily because they were able to hire expensive lawyers who knew the law and the legal system extremely well. Critics praised Kwitny for his powerful book, but a few thought his suggestions for a more just system of justice was naïve.

In 1984 his book *Endless Enemies: The Making of an Unfriendly World* was published. In this book Kwitny examined the nation's foreign policy as it applied to international business. In essence, according to Kwitny, the country's foreign policy looked at foreign countries in terms of communism versus democracy and occasionally supported military forces that opposed communism. Unfortunately, the United States seemed to have a blind eye toward these rogue military forces, especially if their actions caused the economies of the countries in which they fought to tumble.

The Crimes of Patriots: A True Tale of Dope, Dirty Money, and the CIA was published in 1987. This book examined the country's foreign policy and how it related to the operation of the Nugan Hand Bank of Australia, which was an international investment firm that collapsed in 1980. Purportedly, the bank was not only involved in criminal activity, but many of its employees had connections to the United States military and the Central Intelligence Agency (CIA).

Acceptable Risks was published in 1992. Kwitny disclosed how two men smuggled drugs into the country for the purpose of helping those with AIDS. Then they basically pleaded for the Food and Drug Administration (FDA) to speed up the approval process of drugs for AIDS. Kwitny revealed how the FDA seemingly dragged its feet when it came to approving drugs for AIDS.

In 1997 Kwitny's last book, *Man of the Century: The Life and Times of Pope John Paul II*, was published. A biography, Kwitny discussed the pontif's life, including his teachings and his significant role in helping to break up the former Soviet Union.

In addition to writing for *The Wall Street Journal* as well as writing several books, Kwitny hosted "The Kwitny Report," which was broadcast on the Public Broadcasting System (PBS). The program aired a few years.

Kwitny worked for the Gannett newspaper group before he died on November 26, 1998, of stomach cancer.

Representative Works

The Fountain Pen Conspiracy, 1973.
The Mullendore Murder Case, 1974.
Vicious Circles: The Mafia in the Marketplace, 1979.
Endless Enemies: The Making of an Unfriendly World, 1984.
The Crimes of Patriots: A True Tale of Dope, Dirty Money, and the CIA, 1987.
Acceptable Risks, 1992.
Man of the Century: The Life and Times of Pope John Paul II, 1997.

Further Reading

Saxon, Wolfgang. "Jonathan Kwitney, 57, Author and Prize-Winning Reporter." *The New York Times* (28 Nov. 1998).

Weinberg, Steve. "Guts and Accuracy—the Kwitny Trademarks." *The IRE Journal* (Jan.–Feb. 1999).

William Lambert (1920–1998)

Born February 2, 1920, in Langford, South Dakota, William Lambert attended public schools. When he was in high school, he moved with his parents to West Linn, Oregon. Lambert worked as a reporter for the high school newspaper and enjoyed the job so much that he desired to work as a reporter after graduation.

However, he realized that he needed to attend college before he attempted to get a job in journalism. He found employment at a paper mill and had saved several hundred dollars, which was enough to attend college for a year, when World War II erupted in Europe. A member of the National Guard, which was federalized in November 1940, Lambert entered the United States Army as a corporal. He saw at least five major campaigns in the Pacific and was promoted to first lieutenant before he was released five years later.

Upon his discharge from military service, Lambert returned to Oregon, where he married his girlfriend from high school and went to work for the *Oregon City Banner-Courier*, later the *Enterprise-Courier*. Lambert was promoted to news editor before he left the paper in 1950. He joined *The Oregonian* as a police reporter the same year. Together with Wallace Turner, he wrote investigative stories, including a story about Dave Beck, the former president of the Teamsters Union who was involved with questionable individuals and businesses in the Northwest. Beck was investigated by authorities and sentenced to prison, and Lambert and Turner received a Pulitzer Prize in 1957. As a result of their investigative reporting, Lambert and Turner became witnesses before the Senate rackets subcommittee. This action ultimately led both journalists to develop contacts in Washington, D. C.

Lambert received a Nieman Fellowship to Harvard University in 1959. He attended several graduate classes in law, even though he had not attended college.

After his fellowship, Lambert learned that the staff of *The Oregonian* was on strike and that Turner had gotten a job with Abraham Ribicoff in Washington, D. C. Although Turner encouraged Lambert to get a job in Washington, Lambert became an anchor and later a news director at KPTV, a television station in Portland. Within a year, however, he realized television was not for him.

In 1962 he moved to Washington, D. C., where he worked as a press agent for the Office of Education. Working on a per diem basis was not enough to support a family, so he became a correspondent in the Los Angeles bureau of

Time magazine. Lambert was not happy at *Time* because the editors expected precise and concise articles.

In 1963 he learned about *Life* magazine, specifically about the freedom its editors gave to writers who desired to investigate and report at length about controversial subjects. Lambert met with the editor and managing editor of the magazine and persuaded them to hire him as an investigative reporter.

The first major story he wrote for *Life* concerned Lyndon B. Johnson's fortune. Perhaps his biggest story was the incisive article that exposed the relationship between convicted stock manipulator Louis Wolfson and former U. S. Supreme Court Justice Abe Fortas, which appeared in 1969. Fortas had been considered for chief justice by President Johnson, but he resigned from the Supreme Court as a result of the article. Lambert received considerable accolades from his peers for the piece.

Lambert was promoted to an associate editor at *Life* before he left the magazine in 1971. Lambert worked as a correspondent for the Time-Life News Service from 1971 to 1973. Then he worked briefly as a freelance journalist before he joined the staff of *The Philadelphia Inquirer* in 1974, where he remained until 1990.

Lambert died February 8, 1998, in Philadelphia.

Representative Works

Articles, *The Oregonian*.
Articles, *Life*.

Further Reading

Brennan, Elizabeth A., and Elizabeth C. Clarage. "Lambert, William G." *Who's Who of Pulitzer Prize Winners*. Phoenix: Oryx Press, 1999.

Salpukas, Agis. "William Lambert, 78, Writer Who Exposed Justic Fortas." *The New York Times Biographical Service* 29.2 (Feb. 1998).

Gene Marine (1926–2012)

Born December 31, 1926, in San Francisco, Gene Marine served in the United States Marine Corps Reserve from 1943 to 1946. He attended San Francisco State College (now University) from 1948 to 1949.

From 1951 to 1957 Marine worked in news at KPFA, a radio station in Berkeley, California. He also became the West Coast correspondent to *The Nation* in 1954 and contributed numerous articles to the magazine for ten years.

Marine worked as the associate editor of *Frontier* magazine from 1957 to 1959 and then as the program director at KPFK, a radio station in Los Angeles, from 1959 to 1960. He returned to KPFA, in Berkeley, as the news director, where he stayed until 1962.

From 1962 to 1964 he was involved in California politics, first as a campaign manager and then as a member of the Columbia Broadcasting System's (CBS) news staff. In 1964 he became a contributing editor to *Pacific Scene*, a position he held until 1965.

Marine then worked as a senior editor at *Ramparts* magazine in San Francisco for several years. In 1969 he decided he had enough writing experience at radio stations and magazines to become a freelance editor and writer. Although he contributed hundreds of articles to numerous periodicals, his best investigative exposes appeared in books such as *America the Raped: The Engineering Mentality and the Devastation of a Continent*, which was published in 1969, *The Black Panthers*, which was published the same year, and *Food Pollution: The Violation of Our Inner Ecology*, which was co-written with Judith Van Allen and which was published in 1972.

Marine was influenced by Carey McWilliams of *The Nation*. He tried to dismiss stereotypes by concentrating on facts in his articles and especially in his books. Marine explained, "I like books because they give me freedom to tell the truth, which I try to do in a language as clear as is within my command, avoiding political jargon that is as stereotyped as the ideas it would combat."[1]

Marine's *America the Raped: The Engineering Mentality and the Devastation of a Continent*, which explored in-depth the ecological problems caused by technological progress, was timid in its approach. Seldom was forceful language

1 Jane A. Bowden, ed., *Contemporary Authors*, *Vol.* 65–68 (Detroit: Gale Research, 1972), 387.

used to get the author's message across. Whether this approach was appropriate for the topic could be debated. Like *The Black Panthers* and *Food Pollution: The Violation of Our Inner Ecology*, however, it was an honest account of an often distorted subject and therefore an important thought-provoking study.

In 1972 his book *A Male Guide to Women's Liberation* was published.

Marine died in December 2012.

Representative Works

America the Raped: The Engineering Mentality and the Devastation of a Continent, 1969.
The Black Panthers, 1969.
Food Pollution: The Violation of Our Inner Ecology (with Judith Van Allen, 1972.

Further Reading

Marine, Gene. *Contemporary Authors*. Vols. 65–68. Detroit: Gale Research, 1977.
Marine, Gene. *Who's Who in America*. 46th ed., 1990–1991. Wilmette, Ill.: Marquis Who's Who, 1990.
Marine, Gene. *Who's Who in Writers, Editors & Poets, United States & Canada*. 5th ed., 1995–1996. Ed. Curt Johnson. Highland Park, Ill.: December Press, 1995.

John Marks (1943–)

John Marks was born February 21, 1943, to Doris and David Marks in Orange, New Jersey, and attended Cornell University, from which he received his bachelor's degree in 1965.

Marks was hired by the U. S. State Department in 1966 and served in the Foreign Service. Primarily because he would more than likely be drafted for the military, his superiors at the State Department advised him to go to Vietnam as a civilian advisor.[1] Marks reluctantly agreed and served in Vietnam almost two years.

When he returned to the states, he was assigned to the Bureau of Intelligence and Research, where he was introduced to the world of espionage. Marks wrote, "Here I found the same kind of waste and inefficiency I had come to know in Vietnam and, even worse, the same sort of reasoning that had led the country into Vietnam in the first place."[2]

In 1970, after the United States invaded Cambodia, thus escalating the war, Marks left the State Department. He was hired as an executive assistant to Senator Clifford Case of New Jersey, who opposed the war. Marks met Victor Marchetti, who had served in the United States Army in Germany during the early years of the Cold War. When Marchetti left the service, he attended Pennsylvania State University, where he majored in history. He joined the Central Intelligence Agency (CIA) in 1955 and over the years became one of the agency's leading authorities on the Soviet Union. He served as a staff officer in the office of the director of the CIA, where he held several important positions, including executive assistant to the deputy director. Marchetti grew disillusioned with the agency when he realized what the agency's primary function was. According to Marchetti, "Its basic mission was that of clandestine operations, particularly covert action—the secret intervention in the internal affairs of other nations."[3]

Marchetti attempted to expose the agency in a book, but before he wrote one word the agency and the federal government suppressed his efforts. In fact, he was fighting both entities when he met Marks. He explained to Marks, who had a similar interest in intelligence, what had happened. In 1972 he asked Marks to co-write the book.

1 Victor Marchetti and John D. Marks, *The CIA and the Cult of Intelligence* (New York: Alfred A. Knopf, 1974), xiv.

2 Victor Marchetti and John D. Marks, *The CIA and the Cult of Intelligence*, xiv.

3 Victor Marchetti and John D. Marks, *The CIA and the Cult of Intelligence*, xii.

Although *The CIA and the Cult of Intelligence* was ultimately published in 1974, most, if not all, of the passages had to be screened by someone at the CIA. Few books had actually been written about the agency. Fewer still had revealed the internal mechanics. Reviewers claimed the book presented the real purpose of the CIA. For instance, Richard J. Barnet wrote, "It destroys the CIA official cover story, that it has replaced its spies, adventurers, and assassins with rows of Princeton graduates reading foreign newspapers."[4]

Marks and Marchetti had hoped the book would cause some members of Congress to write and pass legislation that would curtail the agency's apparent function, but this did not happen. To this day, CIA operatives work in a climate based on paranoia.

From 1974 to 1978 Marks worked as an associate and then as project director at the Center for National Security Studies in Washington, D. C. While there he and Robert Borosage edited *The CIA File*, which was a collection of papers that had been presented at a conference sponsored by the Center for National Security Studies. The book was published in 1976.

From 1979 until 1981 Marks was at Harvard University, where he was first a fellow at the Institute of Politics of the John F. Kennedy School of Government and then a visiting scholar at the law school as well as a research associate of the Harvard Negotiation Project.

Marks wrote another expose that examined the CIA's counterintelligence operations in the United States during the 1950s and 1960s. Marks provided details of several abuses, including drug experiments and shock treatments, which were part of the CIA's efforts to achieve mind control. He claimed such activities threatened civil liberties. Titled *The Search for the "Manchurian Candidate,"* the book was published in 1979.

Marks worked as a consultant to the Union of Concerned Scientists before he founded the non-profit organization Search for Common Ground in 1982. He founded Common Ground Productions three years later. Both were founded for the purpose of promoting peace. Marks served as president of the organization until 2014.

Marks contributed articles to various publications, including *Playboy*, *The Saturday Review*, *Rolling Stone*, and *Ramparts*.

4 Richard J. Barnet, "Killers and Jokers," *New York Review of Books*, October 3, 1974, 29.

Representative Works

The CIA and the Cult of Intelligence (with Victor Marchetti), 1974.
The Search for the "Manchurian Candidate," 1979.

Further Reading

Marks, John. *Contemporary Authors*. Vol. 110. Detroit: Gale Research, 1984.

Jane Mayer (1955–)

Jane Mayer was born in 1955 to Meredith and William Mayer in New York, New York. She attended Yale University, from which she graduated in 1977. She worked for a few small newspapers in Vermont before she was hired as a reporter by *The Washington Star*.

Mayer joined *The Wall Street Journal* in the early 1980s. As an overseas correspondent, she wrote about the bombing of the United States Marines barracks in Beirut and the Persian Gulf War, among other subjects. Later, she became the newspaper's correspondent at the White House.

Along with Doyle McManus, another journalist, she co-wrote *Landslide: The Unmaking of the President, 1984–1988*, which was published in 1988. The authors examined President Ronald Reagan's second term in office, including his seemingly lack of attention to his administration's questionable activities, including the Iran-Contra affair.

In 1992 Mayer married William Hamilton, who worked as an editor with *The Washington Post* at the time.

With Jill Abramson, Mayer co-wrote the book *Strange Justice: The Selling of Clarence Thomas*, which was published in 1994. The authors discussed Clarence Thomas and his confirmation hearings, including the controversial testimony by Anita Hill, for becoming a justice to the United States Supreme Court.

In 1995 Mayer moved to *The New Yorker*. She wrote about the Democratic Party and the Republican Party. She wrote about several presidents, too.

She wrote *The Dark Side: How the War on Terror Turned into a War on American Ideals*, which was published in 2008. Based on articles she had written for the magazine, the book examined President George W. Bush's administration's handling of the war on terror and the questionable tactics employed on suspected terrorists.

She reported about President Barack Obama's administration's use of drones a year later. In 2010 Mayer discussed how the Koch brothers had used their money over the years to influence Republican politicians in an effort to shape the Republican Party. She returned to the administration of President Barack Obama in 2011, when she examined how the administration was prosecuting whistleblowers.

In 2016 her book *Dark Money: The Hidden History of the Billionaires behind the Rise of the Radical Right* was published. This book, which was based on research she had gathered about the Koch brothers, further explained how the brothers had influenced Republican politicians over the years and consequently the Republican Party. The book also included information about how certain individuals had attempted to discredit the author's journalistic integrity over the years.

Although Mayer's books had been criticized by some and praised by others, more than one writer criticized this book and its author for being naïve. In essence, more than one critic pointed out that both political parties had been influenced and shaped over the years by wealthy individuals and organizations. Indeed, the Democratic Party, like the Republican Party, as one critic mentioned, was no longer the party it once was.

Representative Works

Landslide: The Unmaking of the President, 1984–1988 (with Doyle McManus), 1988.
Strange Justice: The Selling of Clarence Thomas (with Jill Abramson), 1994.
The Dark Side: How the War on Terror Turned into a War on American Ideals, 2008.
Dark Money: The Hidden History of the Billionaires behind the Rise of the Radical Right, 2016.

Further Reading

Jane Mayer. *Gale Literature: Contemporary Authors*. Detroit: Gale, 2016.
Jane Mayer. *The New Yorker* (3 Mar. 2022). www.newyorker.com/contributors/jane-mayer
Langmuir, Molly. "What's Next For *New Yorker* Reporter Jane Mayer?" *Elle* (Mar. 2019).

Gene Edward Miller (1928–2005)

Gene Edward Miller worked as an investigative journalist and later editor at *The Miami Herald* for almost fifty years.

Born on September 16, 1928, to Irene and Paul Miller, in Evansville, Indiana, Miller worked as a copyboy for *The Evansville Press* when he was young. He worked for *The Indiana Daily Student* while working on his bachelor's degree at Indiana University, from which he graduated in 1950.

Miller started his professional career in journalism as a reporter for *The Journal Gazette* in Fort Wayne, Indiana, the same year.

From 1951 to 1953 he served in the United States Army Counter Intelligence Corps during the Korean War. When he was discharged, he returned to journalism, working as a reporter for *The Wall Street Journal*, from which he was fired in 1954. From 1954 to 1957 he worked as a reporter for *The Richmond News Leader*, in Virginia.

Miller moved to *The Miami Herald*, in Florida, in 1957. He worked as a reporter and then as an editor. As a reporter, he covered various subjects, including airline crashes; hurricanes in Haiti; the assassination of President John F. Kennedy in Dallas; the civil rights activities of Dr. Martin Luther King, Jr., in Birmingham, Alabama; the break-in at the Watergate complex and its aftermath; Jim Jones and his mass murder-suicide of almost one thousand men, women, and children in Jonestown, Guyana; the Starr Report and President Bill Clinton; the fire aboard the ship Yarmouth Castle; Senator Ted Kennedy and Chappaquiddick; the shootings at Kent State University; the incident at Three Mile Island; the kidnapping of Patty Hearst; Mai Lai and the Vietnam War; the Attica uprising; Elvis Presley; the murderer Ted Bundy; and Governor George Wallace, to mention several.

Although he covered numerous topics, his award-winning journalism focused primarily on crime. In fact, his reporting about murder helped secure the release of a few individuals from prison. For instance, in 1967 he wrote about Mary Katherin Hampton and Joseph Shea. Both had been convicted of separate killings they had not committed. Mary Katherin had been sentenced to life in prison for two murders. Miller investigated and learned that she had been hundreds of miles away from where the killings had occurred. Miller actually helped Mary Katherin get a new trial. She was released in 1966. Shea had been convicted of killing a reservation clerk in 1959. Miller uncovered evidence that helped Shea get a new trial. He was acquitted and released.

Miller received a Pulitzer Prize for Local Investigative Specialized Reporting in 1967 for these investigative reports. The same year he received a Nieman Fellowship to Harvard University.

Miller, along with Barbara Jane Mackle, co-wrote *Eighty-Three Hours Till Dawn*. The book, which was published in 1971, was based on Mackle's horrible experience of being kidnapped by two individuals who were dressed as police officers and buried alive. The kidnappers demanded $500,000, which was paid. Eventually, Mackle was found. However, the authorities did not find the kidnappers for some time.

Miller received his second Pulitzer Prize for Local General or Spot News Reporting in 1976 for his investigative journalism about a case involving two death-row inmates, Freddie Pitts and Wilbert Lee. These African-American men had been charged in 1963 for allegedly murdering two gas station attendants in Port St. Joe, Florida.

Another man ultimately confessed to the crimes. This information was brought to Miller's attention. Miller wrote more than one hundred articles about the case over several years. He also wrote the book *Invitation to a Lynching*, which was published in 1975. Miller based the book on his investigation and subsequent articles about Freddie Pitts and Wilbert Lee. He revealed the questionable investigation by the police, the contradictory testimony by a primary witness, and the beatings of the accused by the police, which, more than anything else, had caused the men to confess to the crimes and ultimately be sentenced to death.

The numerous articles and proofs of the book were read by the state's attorney general and the governor. As a result of Miller's articles and book, the authorities released Pitts and Lee in 1975.

Miller instinctively understood what topics interested readers. He also knew how to compose sentences that were crisp and direct. Without question, his stories were read with curiosity. As an editor, he helped younger reporters learn how to investigate and write stories readers found interesting. In fact, as a result of his efforts, other journalists writing for the newspaper received awards, including Pulitzer Prizes, for their stories.

Although Miller retired from the newspaper in 2001, he contributed to it from time to time before he died of cancer on June 17, 2005.

Representative Works

Eighty-Three Hours Till Dawn (with Barbara Jane Mackle), 1971.
"The Hampton Case. Frustrating Fight to Free Imprisoned Woman," 1966.
Invitation to a Lynching, 1975.

Further Reading

Downie, Jr., Leonard. *The New Muckrakers*. Washington: New Republic Book Co., 1976.

Dygert, James H. *Investigative Journalist: Folk Heroes of a New Era*. Englewood Cliffs, NJ.: Prentice Hall, 1976.

Fischer, Heinz D. *The Pulitzer Prize Archive: Complete Biographical Encyclopedia of Pulitzer Prize Winners 1917–2000: Journalists, Writers and Composers on Their Way to Coveted Awards*. Vol. 16. Munchen: De Gruyter Saur, 2002.

Stanton, David Duwe. *The Miami Herald and the Miller Effect: Literary Journalism in the 1980s*. Master's Thesis. Gainesville: University of Florida, 2005.

Morton Mintz (1922–)

Investigative journalist Morton Mintz was born January 26, 1922, in Ann Arbor, Michigan, and graduated from the University of Michigan in 1943. He joined the United States Navy and served three years.

Mintz began his career in journalism at the *St. Louis Star-Times* in 1946. An inquisitive reporter who learned how to obtain controversial information, he remained at the *Star-Times* until he was hired by the *St. Louis Globe-Democrat* in 1950. First as a reporter and then as an assistant city editor, Mintz learned various aspects of journalism. He received recognition from his peers when he wrote a series of articles about the mentally handicapped.

In 1958 he moved to Washington, D. C., and became a reporter of merit at *The Washington Post*. Four years later he wrote about thalidomide, which caused deformities in babies. His stories caused a Senate subcommittee to question officials at the Food and Drug Administration. Soon after the hearing the Food and Drug Administration did not approve thalidomide for sale in the United States. Mintz wrote articles about other medicines and medical devices that caused health issues.

However, he did not limit his reporting to just stories and articles for the *Post*. In order to inform more people about what he had uncovered, he wrote *The Therapeutic Nightmare: A Report on Prescription Drugs, the Men Who Make Them, and the Agency that Controls Them*, which was published in 1965, and *By Prescription Only: A Report on the Roles of the United States Food and Drug Administration, the American Medical Association, Pharmaceutical Manufacturers, and Others in Connection with the Irrational and Massive Use of Prescription Drugs that may be Worthless, Injurious, or even Lethal*, which was published in 1967.

These books exposed how drugs were developed and approved by the federal government. However, primarily because of what he had learned, Mintz was critical of the process. Indeed, the federal government had approved certain drugs that had proved harmful. Were pharmaceutical manufacturers too influential in Washington, D. C.?

In 1970 *The Pill: An Alarming Report* was published. This book concerned birth-control pills that had been approved by the federal government for women. Mintz claimed the studies on which the pills were approved by the federal government were lacking careful analysis over time.

With Jerry S. Cohen, Mintz co-wrote *America, Inc.: Who Owns and Operates the United States*, which was published in 1971. The authors wrote

Power, Inc.: Public and Private Rulers and How to Make Them Accountable, which was published in 1976.

Mintz looked at the A. H. Robins Company and the Dalkon Shield, an intrauterine device or IUD, which appeared on the market in 1971, in *At Any Cost: Corporate Greed, Women, and the Dalkon Shield*, which was published in 1985. Mintz examined the company's eagerness to promote and sell the device to generate profits before it proved the device's safety over time. Women who used it suffered from punctured uteri, pelvic infections, abortions, children with birth defects, and unwanted pregnancies. Even though officials of the company realized the product had problems, they refused to take it off the market until it was revealed that the product was unfit for human use.

Although Mintz's previous books were investigative exposes, he and Margaret Mintz wrote *Quotations from President Ron*, which was published in 1987. He and Anita Mintz wrote *President Ron's Appointment Book*, which was published a year later.

Mintz retired from the *Post* in 1988. Two years later he became the chair of the Fund for Investigative Journalism, a position he held for three years.

In 1996 he became a senior advisor to the Nieman Foundation's Watchdog Project, for which he contributed articles that criticized so-called news pundits who appeared on talk shows. In short, Mintz claimed these pundits did not exhibit any journalism ethics. Of course, he criticized others, including executives, who worked for the mainstream media.

Although Mintz has lived a century, he has not stopped writing.

Representative Works

The Therapeutic Nightmare: A Report on Prescription Drugs, the Men Who Make Them, and the Agency that Controls Them, 1965.

By Prescription Only: A Report on the Roles of the United States Food and Drug Administration, the American Medical Association, Pharmaceutical Manufacturers, and Others in Connection with the Irrational and Massive Use of Prescription Drugs that may be Worthless, Injurious, or even Lethal, 1967.

The Pill: An Alarming Report, 1970.

American, Inc.: Who Owns and Operates the United States (with Jerry S. Cohen), 1971.

Power, Inc.: Public and Private Rulers and How to Make Them Accountable (with Jerry S. Cohen), 1976.

At Any Cost: Corporate Greed, Women, and the Dalkon Shield, 1985.

Further Reading

Lieberman, Trudy. "In the Beginning: From a Consumer Movement to Consumerism." *Columbia Journalism Review* 47.3 (Sept.–Oct. 2008).

Mintz, Morton A. *Contemporary Authors*. Vols. 13–16, 1st Rev. Detroit: Gale Research, 1975.

Mintz, Morton Abner. *Who's Who in American Jewry*, 1980 ed. Los Angeles: Standard Who's Who, 1980.

"Morton Mintz to Receive Hefner Award." *The Washington Post* 119 (14 Mar. 1996).

Ralph Nader (1934–)

Born to Rose and Nadra Nader on February 27, 1934, in Winsted, Connecticut, investigative consumer advocate and lawyer Ralph Nader received his bachelor's degree from Princeton University in 1955 and his law degree from Harvard in 1958.

Unlike most students his age, Nader sensed that something was amiss even as an undergraduate. Dwight David Eisenhower was president and the youth were for the most part apathetic. Nader was appalled when he saw students' legal rights stripped by university administrators. Although he tried to interest them in defending their legal rights, he was not successful.[1]

When he left Harvard, Nader served briefly in the United States Army and then practiced law in Hartford, Connecticut. From 1961 to 1967 he taught history and government at the University of Hartford. Although he had written extensively about the failures by the automobile industry to improve its products, it was not until 1964, when he became a consultant to Daniel Patrick Moynihan, then assistant secretary of the U. S. Department of Labor, that his views concerning the federal government's role in implementing laws protecting consumers of automobiles were finally heard. Unfortunately, few politicians, except Moynihan, heeded what he said. Consequently, he turned to writing an investigative report that exposed the ills of America's automobile industry, especially General Motors' Chevrolet Corvair. Titled *Unsafe at Any Speed: The Designed-in Dangers of the American Automobile*, the book was published in 1965 and became one of the most revealing exposes of the decade.

The book influenced Congress to take an active role in regulating the automobile industry, particularly when Nader informed the media that he had been investigated and harassed by detectives hired by General Motors. The president of the company acknowledged the company had conducted an investigation and publicly apologized to Nader. Within six months the National Traffic and Motor Vehicle Safety Act was passed by the U. S. Senate and the U. S. House of Representatives and subsequently signed by President Lyndon Johnson.

Nader had become a one-man lobby for the public. He started to monitor the National Traffic Safety Agency. Eventually, he turned his attention

1 Charles Moritz, ed., *Current Biography Yearbook 1968* (New York: H. W. Wilson, 1968), 279.

to health hazards, including mining, natural gas pipelines, and meat-packing companies, to mention a few.

In 1969 he founded the Center for Study of Responsive Law, which investigated various federal commissions such as the Federal Trade Commission, and in 1970 he initiated the Public Interest Research Group, which worked for consumer and political reform on community and college campuses. In addition to the numerous contributions to magazines and newspapers, Nader and his group of graduate students, law students, and journalists (Nader's Raiders) produced numerous investigative reports on such topics as air pollution, food additives, nursing homes, water pollution, pensions, corporate power, federal agencies, nuclear energy, and banking. He also wrote or co-wrote *What to Do with Your Bad Car*, which was published in 1970, and *Beware*, which was published a year later.

In 1971 Nader launched Public Citizen, Inc., a lobbying organization for consumers, primarily to counteract the power of corporate-sponsored lobbying organizations. He also founded the Center for Auto Safety, the National Insurance Consumer Organization, the Health Research Group, and the Project for Corporate Responsibility.

In 1973 Nader founded the Capitol Hill News Service, primarily to cover the unscrupulous activities of those serving in Congress. A number of investigative reports appeared, including stories about questionable financing for campaigns and bribes in the guise of gifts, trips, and seminars offered to various members of Congress by large lobbying organizations. Although the service was sometimes criticized for its handling of news, it served a public purpose nonetheless.

Nader's organizations influenced the Nixon administration to establish several "watchdog" agencies, including the Occupational Safety and Health Administration, the Environmental Protection Agency, and the Consumer Products Safety Commission. At least eight consumer protection laws were enacted as a result of his organizations' efforts.

When Jimmy Carter became president, many of Nader's protégés were recruited for administrative positions. As a result, Nader's activities were curtailed. Still, he was productive. Between 1973 and 1980 he wrote or co-wrote numerous exposes. These included *You and Your Pension*, *Corporate Power in America*, and *Action for a Change: A Student's Manual for Public Interest Organizing*, which were published in 1973; *Working on the System: A Comprehensive Manual for Citizen Access to Federal Agencies*, which was published in 1974; *Ruling Congress* and *The Ralph Nader Congress Project*, which were published in 1975; *Government Regulation: What Kind of Reform?* and *Taming the Giant Corporation*, which were published in 1976; *The White House* and *The Menace of Atomic Energy*, which were published in 1977; and *The Lemon Book: Auto Rights*, which was published in 1980.

In 1980 Nader resigned as president of Public Citizen, Inc. He founded *The Multinational Monitor*, a magazine that was published for several decades. In addition, he devoted more time to organizing citizens in various communities. A year later he attacked President Ronald Reagan's administration because of its pro-business leanings.

In 1983 Nader founded the U. S. Public Interest Research Group (PIRG), which had support groups in at least twenty-six states. PIRG ultimately helped consumers in states like California to have laws enacted that saved them money on such items as automobile insurance.

Nader's criticism of big business was evident in *The Big Boys: Power and Position in American Business*, which was published in 1986. He and coauthor William Taylor discussed the leading executives of the U. S. Steel Corporation, General Motors, and other corporations. The subjects were thoroughly researched. Two years later he persuaded celebrities such as Dustin Hoffman and Paul Newman, among others, to demonstrate publicly the inflate-on-impact air bag for cars. He also wrote an article of advice to the next president of the United States, which was published in the *Harvard Business Review*.

In 1990 Nader and Wesley J. Smith's *Winning the Insurance Game: The Complete Consumer's Guide to Saving Money* was published. The authors detailed the major types of insurance, including government programs such as Social Security and Medicare, and instructed consumers on how to work with agents, policies, and forms. Three years later he and Wesley J. Smith's *Collision Course: The Truth about Aviation Safety* was published. The authors used interviews, documented reports, and crash accounts, among other evidence, to illustrate their concerns about the discrepancies in the information regarding airline safety, air traffic control, and the airline industry's equipment. Nader and Wesley J. Smith's *No Contest: How the Power Lawyers are Perverting Justice in America* was published in 1996.

Nader ran for president of the United States in 1996 and 2000 as a Green Party candidate. Four years later he ran as a Reform Party candidate. In 2008 he ran as an independent. Although he did not win each time he ran, he brought attention to issues that the mainstream media often overlooked.

Surprisingly, Nader called for President Barack Obama to be impeached because of his military intervention in Libya in 2011. Of course, the U. S. House of Representatives ignored him.

His book *Told You So*, a collection of weekly columns about the numerous problems confronting the United States, including the effects of corporate power and commercialism, among others, on individuals was published in 2013.

A year later he started co-hosting a radio program on which prominent movers and shakers were interviewed. Although the program originated in Los Angeles, it was distributed to other stations.

In 2015 Nader founded the American Museum of Tort Law in Winsted, Connecticut.

Nader continues to write or co-write books that raise eyebrows. For instance, he and Mark Green's *Wrecking America: How Trump's Lawbreaking and Lies Betray All*, which discussed President Donald Trump in negative terms, was published in 2020.

Representative Works

Unsafe at Any Speed: The Designed-in Dangers of the American Automobile, 1965.
Beware, 1971.
You and Your Pension (with Kate Blackwell), 1973.
Corporate Power in America (with Mark Green), 1973.
Ruling Congress, 1975.
Government Regulation: What Kind of Reform?, 1976.
Taming the Giant Corporation, 1976.
The Menace of Atomic Energy (with John Abbotts), 1977.
The Lemon Book: Auto Rights, 1980.
The Big Boys: Power and Position in American Business (with William Taylor), 1986.
Collision Course: The Truth about Aviation Safety (with Wesley J. Smith), 1993.
No Contest: How the Power Lawyers are Perverting Justice in America (with Wesley J. Smith), 1996.

Further Reading

Acton, Jay. *Ralph Nader: A Man and a Movement*. New York: Warner Books, 1972.
Brimelow, Peter, and Leslie Spencer. "Ralph Nader, Inc." *Forbes* 146 (17 Sept. 1990).
Graham, Kevin. *Ralph Nader: Battling for Democracy*. Denver: Windom Publishing Co., 2000.
Green, Mark. "Nader Then and Now." *Nation* 301.25–26 (21 Dec. 2015).
"The Life and Legacy of Ralph Nader." *US Official News*, 15 Aug. 2018.
Marcello, Patricia Cronin. *Ralph Nader: A Biography*. Westport, Ct.: Greenwood Press, 2004.

McGarry, Charles. *Citizen Nader*. New York: Saturday Review Press, 1972.

McGuire, William, and Leslie Wheeler. *American Social Leaders*. Santa Barbara, Cal.: ABC-CLIO, 1993.

Nader, Ralph. *Current Biography*. New York: The H. W. Wilson Co., 1986.

Trachtenberg, Sarah. "Ralph Nader." *Dictionary of Literary Biography, Vol. 345, American Radical and Reform Writers*, Second Series. Ed. Hester Lee Furey. Detroit: Gale Cengage Learning, 2009.

Jack Nelson (1929–2009)

Investigative reporter Jack Nelson was born in Talladega, Alabama, on October 11, 1929, and briefly attended Georgia State College (now University). After writing news releases for the United States Army, his career as a hardnosed and inquisitive reporter began in 1947, in Mississippi, with the *Biloxi Daily Herald*, for which he wrote about illegal gambling payoffs and slot machine concessions. Although his life was threatened more than once, he did not stop his investigations.

In 1952 Nelson joined the staff of the *Atlanta Constitution*, one of the better newspapers of the South, and wrote investigative stories for more than a dozen years. Several of the stories concerned vice and corruption in Liberty County, Georgia, and led to twenty-two indictments. Another series of articles concerned Milledgeville Central State Hospital, which served the mentally ill. Nelson uncovered various abuses, including nurses performing major surgeries on patients and doctors conducting experimental treatments on patients without their consent. As a result of Nelson's series, major changes were made at the hospital. Nelson received a Pulitzer Prize in 1960.

In 1963 he and Gene Roberts, Jr., wrote the in-depth study *The Censors and the Schools*, which revealed how certain pressure groups tried to influence the selection and content of textbooks.

Two years later Nelson joined the *Los Angeles Times* as the chief of the newspaper's Atlanta bureau. In 1970 he moved to Washington, D. C., to work at the newspaper's Washington bureau. Within a few months his curiosity had caused a tremor. When he wrote a revealing story about the FBI and its director, J. Edgar Hoover, the director immediately notified the management of the *Times* that Nelson should be fired. Although Hoover, in most cases, could have gotten his wish earlier in his career, he failed to persuade the newspaper's management in this instance. On the other hand, Nelson came across another interesting operation that had been performed by the FBI. Apparently, the FBI had paid criminal informants thousands of dollars to set up two Ku Klux Klan hit-men in Meridian, Mississippi. The authorities caught the hit-men attempting to plant a bomb in a Jewish man's home and a shootout ensued. After the weapons stopped firing, the authorities learned that one of the hit-men who had been killed was actually a woman. According to John C. Behrens, "The setup had become, in fact, an execution."[1]

1 John C. Behrens, *The Typewriter Guerrillas: Closeups of 20 Top Investigative Reporters*

Of course, none of those involved in the case—the FBI, the Meridian police, the Meridian Jewish community, and the Anti-Defamation League—wanted the story published, but the 6,000-word article appeared in the *Los Angeles Times* anyway.

Nelson continued his investigations for the newspaper. He also continued to write insightful books. For instance, *The Orangeburg Massacre*, which was written with Jack Bass, another investigative reporter, was published in 1970. The authors examined the 1968 protest against segregation by African-American students on the campus of South Carolina State College (now University). More than two dozen were shot by the authorities. Three died. The authors disclosed the truth about the whitewashed murders of the three students.

Two years later Nelson and Ronald J. Ostrow's book *The FBI and the Berrigans: The Making of a Conspiracy* was published. The Berrigans, who were brothers and Catholic priests, opposed the war in Vietnam. They recruited several others who had similar beliefs and subsequently plotted to blow up steam pipes that provided heat to federal buildings in Washington, D. C., and kidnap Henry Kissinger, the security advisor to President Richard Nixon. However, most of those involved, including one of the brothers, were charged by the authorities before they could execute their plan. Nelson and Ostrow's book covered the trial of the accused.

Nelson turned his attention to high school journalism in *Captive Voices: The Report of the Commission of Inquiry into High School Journalism in America*, which was published in 1974.

A year later Nelson became chief of the Washington bureau. Although his duties included administrative and reporting assignments, he performed exceptionally well at both. His preference was, of course, reporting.

Nelson wrote the insightful *Terror in the Night: The Klan's Campaign Against the Jews*, which was published in 1993. The book was based on information he had uncovered years earlier that resulted in the several thousand-word story mentioned above. In the book Nelson described the Ku Klux Klan's anti-Semitic beliefs as well as the Klan's plan to bomb the home of Meyer Davidson, a community leader who had been outspoken about the synagogue bombings in Mississippi. Nelson explained that the Klan hated the Jews primarily because they believed the Jews had been responsible for inciting civil rights for African Americans. Nelson described the setup as well as

(Chicago: Nelson-Hall, 1966), 172.

the ambush of Thomas Albert Tarrants III and Kathy Ainsworth. The FBI, which had informants inside the Klan, and officers of the local police department were at the scene when Tarrants and Ainsworth were about to plant a bomb. In the ensuing battle, Ainsworth was killed. Tarrants was arrested and ultimately sentenced to prison. The book was thoroughly researched and extremely well-written.

Nelson stepped down as bureau chief in 1996, but served as the newspaper's chief correspondent in Washington until he retired in 2001. He died of cancer October 21, 2009.

His memoir, *Scoop: The Evolution of a Southern Reporter*, which was edited by Barbara Matusow, his wife, was published in 2012.

Representative Works

The Censors and the Schools (with Gene Roberts), 1963.
The Orangeburg Massacre (with Jack Bass), 1970.
The FBI and the Berrigans: The Making of a Conspiracy (with Ronald J. Ostrow), 1972.
Terror in the Night: The Klan's Campaign Against the Jews, 1993.

Further Reading

Brennan, Elizabeth A., and Elizabeth C. Clarage. "Nelson, John Howard." *Who's Who of Pulitzer Prize Winners*. Phoenix: Oryx Press, 1999.

Nelson, Jack. *Contemporary Authors*. Vol. 292. Detroit: Gale, Cengage Learning, 2010.

Nelson, Jack. *Scoop: The Evolution of a Southern Reporter*. Ed. Barbara Matusow. Jackson, Miss.: University Press of Mississippi, 2013.

Bernard Nossiter (1926–1992)

Born on April 10, 1926, to Rose and Murray Nossiter in New York City, investigative economics journalist Bernard Nossiter received his bachelor's degree from Dartmouth College in 1947 and his master's degree from Harvard a year later.

In 1952 he went to work as a reporter for *The New York World Telegram and Sun*. Concurrently, he started contributing articles that he believed were too controversial for any newspaper to *The Nation*.

In 1955 he became the national economics reporter for *The Washington Post*, a position he held until 1964. From 1964 to 1979 he served as an economics correspondent for the newspaper. He was stationed in Paris and then Asia and then London before he moved to *The New York Times* in 1979. Soon, he became the head of the newspaper's bureau at the United Nations.

In addition to his work for *The New York Times* and his articles for *The Nation* and other periodicals, Nossiter wrote the critical and analytical *The Mythmakers: An Essay on Power and Wealth*, which was published in 1964. Nossiter explained the economic policies of President John F. Kennedy and argued that the United States should emulate Japan and France in planning its economic future. *Soft State: A Newspaperman's Chronicle of India* followed in 1970.

Britain—A Future That Works was published in 1978 and argued that England's growth would rely on its varied cultural skills rather than on its manufacturing firms. Nossiter's arguments regarding England differed greatly from those of most political and economic observers at the time.

The Global Struggle for More: Third World Conflicts with Rich Nations, which was published in 1987, examined the progression of the Third World after World War II. Basically, Nossiter attacked foreign aid and argued that tough policy conditions should be attached to World Bank loans to poor countries.

Nossiter's last book was *Fat Years and Lean: The American Economy Since Roosevelt*. Published in 1990, the book was a chatty account of American economic policy-making from the Depression to the present. Nossiter discussed the people who were responsible for the decisions, including their intellectual and class perspectives as well as the positions they took on whether and how to fight unemployment. He criticized supply-side economics as well as the conservatives who supported the theory. He also criticized big labor and President Ronald Reagan.

Nossiter died of cancer in 1992.

Representative Works

The Mythmakers: An Essay on Power and Wealth, 1964.
Britain—A Future That Works, 1978.
The Global Struggle for More: Third World Conflicts with Rich Nations, 1987.
Fat Years and Lean: The American Economy Since Roosevelt, 1990.

Further Reading

Nossiter, Bernard D. *Contemporary Authors*. Vols. 41–44, 1st Rev. Detroit: Gale Research, 1979.
Nossiter, Bernard D(aniel). *Contemporary Authors*. Vol. 138. Detroit: Gale Research, 1993.
Smith, J. Y. "Bernard D. Nossiter, 66, Dies; Economics Reporter, Author." *The Washington Post* 115 (25 June 1992).

Miriam Ottenberg (1914–1982)

Born on October 7, 1914, to Nettie and Louis Ottenberg, in Washington, D. C., Miriam attended Central High School in the nation's capital, from which she graduated in 1931.

Ottenberg attended Goucher College for two years and then transferred to the University of Wisconsin-Madison. Although she worked for the university newspaper, *The Daily Cardinel*, before she earned a bachelor's degree in 1935, she found a job as a copywriter at Neisser-Meyerhoff, an advertising agency in Chicago, after she graduated.

Ottenberg worked for the agency about a year and then worked as a reporter for the *Akron Times-Press* in Ohio. She returned to her hometown in 1937 to work for *The Washington Evening Star*.

At first, Ottenberg wrote about public service organizations and their activities. She also wrote human-interest stories that editors thought would appeal to readers. Within two or three years she was covering hard news, especially murders that occurred in the city.

When the United States entered World War II, she wrote stories about the military draft and investigated the federal disaster assistance and civil defense programs. After the war, she focused primarily on crime. Between 1951 and 1959 she was recognized several times by the Washington Newspaper Guild for her articles about crime. In 1958 local and federal officials, including the police, held a banquet in her honor primarily because she had exposed various criminal activities, including murder, and had helped fight it with her words.

She received a Pulitzer Prize for Local Reporting in 1960 for her seven-part series "Buyer Beware." This series concerned used car dealerships and their fraudulent practices. Unsuspecting customers were not necessarily aware of the practices these businesses employed to sell cars. Ottenberg uncovered other kinds of consumer fraud, too. For instance, she wrote the series "Homeowners Beware" in 1960, "Investors Beware" in 1962, and "Debtor Beware" in 1969. Of course, she wrote other series and stories, including a first-hand investigative report about baby brokers who swindled married couples who were interested in adopting children.

In 1962 her book *The Federal Investigators* was published. Robert F. Kennedy, who was the Attorney General at the time, wrote the foreword. Filled with intrigue, the book presented candid information about seventeen agencies of the federal government that investigated criminal activity

A year later she was the first reporter in the country to write about Joe Valachi, a member of the Cosa Nostra or Mafia, who informed the authorities about the organized crime network or syndicate.

As a result of her numerous articles about criminal activities, new laws were written and enacted. She argued for stronger laws pertaining to narcotics as well.

Ottenberg also wrote about juvenile delinquency, the Secret Service, political corruption, bank robbers, religious scams or fraud, phony marriage counselors, chain letter schemes, gambling, labor racketeering, fraudulent charities, scams or fraud pertaining to prizes, a multi-state abortion ring, stock fraud, securities fraud, psychopaths, and dope addicts. She even wrote about the U. S. Postal Service being used for sending obscene material.

In addition to writing for the newspaper, she wrote articles for *U. S. News & World Report*, *Look*, and the *New Republic*.

Unfortunately, Ottenberg had contracted multiple sclerosis when she was younger but had not been diagnosed until years later. She retired from the newspaper in 1974 primarily because of her health. She investigated the disease and wrote articles about it. Then she interviewed others who had the disease and wrote the book *The Pursuit of Hope*, which was published in 1978. The book presented the battle against the disease that she and others fought. The book was extremely positive and well received.

Ottenberg died of cancer in November 1982.

Representative Works

"Anatomy of bank robbery," 1965.
"Buyer Beware," 1960.
"Debtor Beware," 1969.
The Federal Investigators, 1962.
"Homeowners Beware," 1960.
"In the Nation's Capital, crisis in crime," 1965.
"Investors Beware," 1962.
"A Long Look at Gangland," 1962.
"What's Ahead for the FBI," 1965.

Further Reading

Carper, Elsie. "Reporter Miriam Ottenberg of the *Washington Star* Dies," *The Washington Post* 105 (10 Nov 1982).

Dygert, James H. *The Investigative Journalist: Folk Heroes of a New Era*. Englewood Cliffs, NJ.: Prentice-Hall, 1976.

Hoyt, Kendall K. *Drunk Before Noon: the Behind-the-Scenes Story of the Washington Press Corps*. Englewood Cliffs, NJ.: Prentice-Hall, 1979.

Marzolf, Marion. *Up from the Footnote: A History of Women Journalists*. New York: Hastings House, 1977.

Miriam Ottenberg. *Gale Literature: Contemporary Authors*. Detroit: Gale, 2007.

Thomas Powers (1940–)

Investigative reporter Thomas Powers was born on December 12, 1940, in New York City. He graduated from Yale University in 1964, and for two years worked as a reporter at the *Rome Daily American* in Rome, Italy. When he returned to New York City, he worked as a reporter for the United Press International (UPI).

Powers, together with Lucinda Franks, another reporter at UPI, wrote several stories about Diana Oughton under the descriptive title "Making of a Terrorist." Diana Oughton had graduated from Bryn Mawr College and had joined the radical group, Weather Underground. The Weather Underground employed acts of violence whenever its members demonstrated against the Vietnam War. In fact, Oughton and a few others were killed when the bomb they were making exploded in their apartment. Powers and Franks received a Pulitzer Prize for their stories in 1971.

Powers included additional information about Diana Oughton in *Diana: The Making of a Terrorist*, which was published in 1971. Indeed, he explored the numerous unpredictable causes for Oughton's tragic ending.

Powers left UPI so he could write articles for periodicals and books. In 1973, in *The War at Home: Vietnam and the American People, 1964–68*, he examined in-depth the societal and attitudinal changes of the American people toward the Vietnam War.

Perhaps his most important investigative piece of nonfiction was published in 1979. Titled *The Man Who Kept the Secrets: Richard Helms and the CIA*, the book revealed the questionable subversive operations of the Central Intelligence Agency (CIA) that occurred while Helms was associated with the agency. Powers questioned the agency's role in the world—a role he believed had become a problem. In the book's introduction, Powers discussed four aspects of the problem:

(1) American intervention in foreign countries always matters more to the nation in question than it does to the United States. Yet the decision to proceed is often reached in a manner which is shockingly casual....

(2) Just as American power has more sway in other countries than it can claim by right, local CIA officers exert a disproportionate influence on local events, especially after a decision to intervene has been reached....

(3) The CIA has been too quick to surrender responsibility for what allies undertake with its aid, and other high officials in Washington have been too ready to let it do so....

(4) Perhaps the most troubling aspect of the CIA is the hardest to explain, because it represents at once both the field of its greatest success and its passive acceptance of fatal dangers about which there is very likely nothing to be done...[1]

Powers focused his attention on Helms and the various clandestine operations performed by members of the agency. As he described these operations and the people involved, he explained how the operations related to the four aspects mentioned above. Although Powers was somewhat poetic in his descriptions of the various relationships between the executive branch of the federal government and the CIA, his writing was clear and understandable. Consequently, the reader had no difficulty in learning about a complex subject.

Powers contributed a series of essays to *Commonweal* magazine between 1976 and 1982. He collected these essays in *Thinking about the Next War*, which was published in 1982. Powers suggested that a limited nuclear war was inevitable. (The reader should remember that the United States and the former Soviet Union were engaged in a Cold War at the time.) Powers discussed the various forces that drove societies toward nuclear obliteration as well as the effects of this prospect on the minds of parents and their children.

Powers became a contributing editor at *The Atlantic Monthly*. In addition to writing articles for this magazine, he continued to write articles for other periodicals as well as books. He examined the German physicist Werner Heisenberg as well as Nazi Germany's failure to produce an atomic bomb in *Heisenberg's War: The Secret History of the German Bomb*, which was published in 1993. According to Powers, the Nazi leaders paid scant attention to what other countries were doing in nuclear physics. The program that had been started in Nazi Germany in 1939 was abruptly halted in 1942, when Heisenberg informed Albert Speer that an atomic bomb could not be produced fast enough to alter the course of the war. Powers recounted the United States' attempts to learn what was occurring inside Heisenberg's laboratories in Berlin and Leipzig. The book was thoroughly researched and well-written.

In 2000 *The Confirmation*, a novel, was published.

1 Thomas Powers, *The Man Who Kept the Secrets: Richard Helms and the CIA* (New York: Alfred A. Knopf, 1979), viii–x.

His next book, however, was nonfiction. Titled *Intelligence Wars: American Secret History from Hitler to Al-Qaeda*, the book was published in 2002. Powers clearly presented the history of the federal government's efforts to gather intelligence about leaders and their administrations in other countries from the early 1900s to the early 2000s.

The Military Error: Baghdad and Beyond in America's War of Choice followed in 2008. In this book Powers examined how the CIA made a grave mistake when its operatives claimed Saddam Hussein, the leader of Iraq, had weapons of mass destruction. This claim, perhaps more than any other, was the excuse given by President George W. Bush to start the war in Iraq. As it turned out, Hussein did not have any such weapons.

Powers wrote about the past in *The Killing of Crazy Horse*, which was published in 2010. The book is filled with numerous whites and American Indians, including Crazy Horse who defeated General Custer at the battle of Little Big Horn in 1876. Unfortunately, after the federal authorities had taken Crazy Horse into custody, he died. Powers presented Crazy Horse's life as well as the events that led up to his death.

Representative Works

Diana: The Making of a Terrorist, 1971.
The War at Home: Vietnam and the American People, 1964–68, 1973.
The Man Who Kept the Secrets: Richard Helms and the CIA, 1979.
Heisenberg's War: The Secret History of the German Bomb, 1993.
Intelligence Wars: American Secret History from Hitler to Al-Qaeda, 2002.
The Military Error: Baghdad and Beyond in America's War of Choice, 2008.
The Killing of Crazy Horse, 2010.

Further Reading

Powers, Thomas. *World Authors: 1995–2000*. Ed. Clifford Thompson and Mari Rich. New York: H. W. Wilson Co., 2003.

Powers, Thomas. *Contemporary Authors, New Revision Series*. Vol. 15. Detroit: Thomson Gale, 2006.

Powers, Thomas. *Contemporary Authors, New Revision Series*. Detroit: Gale, Cengage Learning, 2012.

James Ridgeway (1936–2021)

James Ridgeway was born on November 1, 1936, in Auburn, New York, and was educated at Princeton University, from which he received his bachelor's degree in 1959.

He began his career as a journalist with *The Wall Street Journal*, where he learned to write concise and accurate stories on the economic conditions of the United States. From 1962 to 1968 he worked as an investigative reporter for *The New Republic*. Ridgeway gathered information from industrial, educational, and governmental reports and then wrote exposes on such subjects as water pollution, auto safety, unethical business practices, and the energy crisis.

In 1968 he and Andrew Kopkind founded and edited *Mayday*, which ultimately became *Hard Times*, a Washington-based journal that exposed industrial and governmental corruption. The same year Ridgeway's controversial *The Closed Corporation: American Universities in Crisis* was published. Ridgeway claimed that American universities, especially the research universities, had changed into military and industrial institutions rather than educational institutions because of the research professors were conducting. According to Ridgeway, the research was for the government and industry.

Ridgeway's study appeared when students were calling for more power on campuses and revealed that certain institutions such as the Massachusetts Institute of Technology and Johns Hopkins University were involved in developing military weapons, including missiles. Other major universities were involved in other forms of military research.

From 1970 to 1974 Ridgeway worked as an associate editor of *Ramparts*, which published investigative exposes. In his second book-length study, *The Politics of Ecology*, which was published in 1970, Ridgeway first exposed the environmental pollution by industries, particularly the petroleum industry, and then claimed the laws failed to prosecute or even fine the companies responsible. In fact, according to Ridgeway, the laws favored the polluters by allowing the companies to exploit natural resources and by providing tax breaks for their efforts.

Ridgeway became a staff writer as well as a political columnist for *The Village Voice* in 1974. He became the paper's Washington correspondent several years later, a position he held for more than thirty years. He also contributed articles to several periodicals, including *Parade* and *Rolling Stone*. In addition to writing several books or guides on energy-efficient living, he wrote the investigative expose *The Last Play: The Struggle to Monopolize the World's*

Energy Resources, which was published in 1973. The book concerned pork barreling in the oil industry by such oil cartels as Mobil, Gulf, Texaco, and Shell. He wrote *Who Owns the Earth?*, which was published in 1980. The book discussed the development of energy from renewable sources.

Ridgeway edited *The March to War*, which was published in 1991 and which was an anthology of articles, transcripts of press briefings, congressional hearings, and outpourings from such luminaries as Henry Kissinger and Pat Buchanan about the Gulf War. He wrote *Blood in the Face: The Ku Klux Klan, Aryan Nations, Nazi Skinheads, and the Rise of a New White Culture*, which was published in 1991. Ridgeway explored several racist organizations and the ugly atrocities perpetrated by their members on innocent individuals.

Ridgeway and Jean Casella edited *Cast a Cold Eye: The Best in American Opinion Writing, 1990–1991*, which was published in 1992. The essays were from prominent newspapers and magazines and discussed Clarence Thomas, the U. S. invasion of Panama, and childcare, among other topics of the day. Ridgeway wrote *Red Light: Inside the Sex Industry*, which was published in 1996. The book explored the sex industry in the United States. In fact, Ridgeway interviewed actors, prostitutes, strippers, and topless dancers, among others, and learned that some interviewees believed they were working in a socially valuable profession. Others found their work personally empowering. Sylvia Plachy, a photographer, provided photographs for the book.

It's All for Sale: The Control of Global Resources was published in 2004 and revealed which companies owned which products, which companies purchased which products, and which companies sold which products. According to Ridgeway, there were numerous companies all over the world, but most of the products used by people every day were made and sold by fewer and fewer companies seemingly every year.

A year later *The 5 Unanswered Questions about 9/11: What the 9/11 Commission Report Failed to Tell Us* was published. In this book Ridgeway examined the 9/11 Commission Report, which was declared to be the definitive account of the horrific attack that killed several thousand American lives on American soil, and raised other questions that should have been asked by members of the commission and answered.

Ridgeway left *The Village Voice* in 2006. He headed the Washington bureau of *Mother Jones*, a periodical, until 2012. In addition to his duties for *Mother Jones*, he founded Solitary Watch in 2009, a nonprofit group that investigated solitary confinement in jails and prisons across the country.

His book *Blood in the Face: White Nationalism from the Birth of a Nation to the Age of Trump* was published in 2019. The book presented the histories of various violent organizations, including the Ku Klux Klan and the John Birch Society, among others, that had been founded in the United States. Although the mainstream media had claimed these groups and others had led to the more recent radical white supremacy movement, including members of the Republican Party, such organizations had been founded by members of the Democratic Party, not the Republican Party. (Many so-called journalists working today do not know their country's history or intentionally mislead their readers, listeners, or viewers.)

Ridgeway died in 2021.

Representative Works

Mayday (Cofounder and Editor).
Hard Times (Founder and Editor).
The Closed Corporation: American Universities in Crisis, 1968.
The Politics of Ecology, 1970.
The Last Play: The Struggle to Monopolize the World's Energy Resources, 1971.
Who Owns the Earth?, 1980.
Blood in the Face: The Ku Klux Klan, Aryan Nations, Nazi Skinheads, and the Rise of a New White Culture, 1991.
Red Light: Inside the Sex Industry (with Sylvia Plachy, photographer), 1996.
It's All for Sale: the Control of Global Resources, 2004.
The 5 Unanswered Questions about 9/11: What the 9/11 Commission Report Failed to Tell Us, 2005.
Blood in the Face: White Nationalism from the Birth of a Nation to the Age of Trump, 2019.

Further Reading

Dorgan, Charity Anne. "James Ridgeway." *Gale Literature: Contemporary Authors*. Detroit: Gale, 2021.

Langer, Emily. "James Ridgeway, Muckraking Journalist of the Old School, Dies at 84." *The Washington Post* (16 Feb. 2021).

McFadden, Robert D. "James Ridgeway, a Journalist Who Attacked Skulduggery, Is Dead at 84." *The New York Times* (15 Feb. 2021).

Ridgeway, James. *Contemporary Authors*. Vol. 106. Detroit: Gale Research, 1982.

Raquel Rutledge (1960–)

Born in the late 1960s in Milwaukee, Wisconsin, Raquel Rutledge graduated from Shorewood High School in Shorewood, Wisconsin. She received her bachelor's degree from the University of Wisconsin-Milwaukee.

Rutledge worked at *The Freeman* in Waukesha, Wisconsin, before she moved to *The Gazette* in Colorado Springs, Colorado, where she remained almost seven years. She moved to the *Milwaukee Journal Sentinel* in 2004.

She has written about various topics, including lead poisoning in children, high levels of mercury in sushi, ethanol, dishonest mechanics, dirty gasoline, safety issues, public health, tax issues, the Bureau of Alcohol, Tobacco, Firearms, and Explosives, and numerous other subjects.

Her investigative journalism has taken as long as one or two years. Assigned to the newspaper's Public Investigator team, Rutledge has investigated "Wisconsin Shares," which is the state's child-care program for low-income parents. Titled "Cashing in on Kids," the series revealed widespread fraud and criminal activity that not only failed the children, but cost taxpayers millions and millions of dollars. The series caused the state to investigate and issue indictments. The series also was responsible for the state legislature to enact laws that prevented such illegal activity from happening again in the program. As a result of the series, Rutledge received the Pulitzer Prize for Local Reporting and the Goldsmith Prize for Investigative Reporting in 2010. The series earned other awards as well.

In 2011 she received a Nieman Fellowship at Harvard University and studied regulations pertaining to food.

A year later she led the investigation that resulted in the series "A Case of Shattered Trust," which concerned tainted alcohol sanitary wipes that had been distributed by a company in Wisconsin. The series earned a Gerald Loeb Award in 2012.

Rutledge and John Diedrich, another investigative journalist, investigated a nationwide sting operation initiated by agents of the Bureau of Alcohol, Tobacco, Firearms and Explosives. The journalists' investigation produced the eye-opening series "Backfire," which concerned the operation. The investigative journalists learned the agents had opened gun- and drug-buying stores and had employed individuals who were mentally handicapped. Several of these individuals had used drugs. Then the agents had charged these individuals with crimes. This series received the top award from the Investigative Reporters and Editors (IRE) organization in 2014.

In 2014 she and another investigative reporter investigated the disparity in property taxes in the lengthy series "Trouble with Taxes." Receiving an O'Brien Fellowship in Public Service Journalism at Marquette University, Rutledge, with help from a few others, was responsible for the series "Gasping for Action" in 2015. The series explained how a chemical was endangering people who roasted coffee beans as well as people who used e-cigarettes.

Three years later she produced investigative articles about tourists staying in resorts in Mexico and being poisoned by tainted alcoholic drinks. Several individuals were injured while others died.

In 2020 Rutledge led the investigation that resulted in the series "In the Shadows," which was about healthcare workers and the violence they encountered while working at their jobs.

During the fall of 2021 she was a Visiting Distinguished Professor at the University of Arkansas in Fayetteville.

Representative Works

"Cashing in on Kids," 2009.
"Shattered Trust," 2012.
"Backfire," 2013.
"Trouble with Taxes," 2014.
"Gasping for Action," 2015.
"In the Shadows," 2020.

Further Reading

Katches, Mark. "Investing in Watchdog Reporting. '... the *Journal Sentinel* has built a 10-person Watchdog Team with a robust Web presence called Watchdog Online.'" *Nieman Reports* 62.3 (Fall 2008).

"Pulitzer Prize-Winning Journalist to Lecture on Ethics in Journalism." *States News Service* (21 Sept. 2021).

"Raquel Rutledge of *Milwaukee Journal Sentinel* Wins Goldsmith Prize for Investigative Reporting." *States News Service* (24 Mar. 2010).

Rector, Kevin. "Watchdogs with Teeth: A *Milwaukee Journal Sentinel* Team Focuses on Accountability Reporting." *American Journalism Review* 30.3 (June–July 2008).

Robert Sherrill (1924–2014)

Born in Frogtown, Georgia, on December 24, 1924, Robert Sherrill earned a bachelor's degree from what is now Pepperdine University in 1949 and a master's degree in English from the University of Texas at Austin in 1956. He earned a second master's in library science from the University of Minnesota four years later.

Sherrill worked at several newspapers until 1954. He also taught at what is now Texas A & M University and the University of Missouri. He returned to journalism in 1960, when he joined the staff at *The Texas Observer*. Sherrill, along with such journalists as Ronnie Dugger, Willie Morris, and Larry L. King, informed readers about state politics. They also wrote in-depth articles that explored the political process in the nation's capital.

After three years, Sherrill moved to *The Miami Herald*, where he was made chief of the capital bureau in Tallahassee. Two years later he moved to Washington, D.C., where he worked for *The Nation*. For this publication, he served as a White House correspondent, a Washington correspondent, and a corporations correspondent. He left the publication in the early 2000s.

In addition, he wrote articles for *Esquire*, *Harper's*, *Penthouse*, *Playboy*, *The New York Times Magazine*, and *The Washington Post*, among other magazines.

Sherrill's experiences in the nation's capital enabled him to write several exposes. For instance, *The Accidental President*, which was a critical biography of President Lyndon Johnson, was published in 1967. *Military Justice Is to Justice as Military Music Is to Music* followed in 1970. This book provided a vivid account of how the military dispensed justice to those charged. *Why They Call It Politics: A Guide to America's Government* was published in 1972 and featured a disturbing portrait of those elected to serve their country. *The Saturday Night Special, and Other Guns with Which Americans Won the West, Protected Bootleg Franchises, Slew Wildlife, Robbed Countless Banks, Shot Husbands Purposely and by Mistake, and Killed Presidents* followed a year later and criticized the lobbying organization of the National Rifle Association as well as the gun-control advocates who believed that legislation could actually solve an age-old problem.

In 1974, in an article that appeared in *The New York Times Magazine*, Sherrill revealed to readers that the existing evidence of the 1969 Chappaquiddick drowning of Mary Jo Kopechne contradicted Senator Edward Kennedy's account. Sherrill criticized journalists for failing to conduct a thorough investigation. Two years later his book *The Last Kennedy: Edward M.*

Kennedy of Massachusetts, Before and After Chappaquiddick, which concerned Ted Kennedy's life, was published.

Eventually, Sherrill devoted more time to writing articles and books and less time to *The Nation*. In addition to writing about politics, he examined other subjects such as the petroleum industry. For instance, he wrote *The Oil Follies of 1970–1980: How the Petroleum Industry Stole the Show (And Much More Besides)*, which was published in 1983. The book provided in-depth details about the oil industry during the previous decade.

Perhaps Sherrill's most insightful expose concerned politics in the South. First published in 1968, *Gothic Politics in the Deep South: Stars of the New Confederacy* was revised in 1969 and again in 1991. The book provided in-depth and critical portraits of the various racists who had become leaders of the so-called New Confederacy states, including Louisiana, Mississippi, Arkansas, Alabama, and Georgia.

Sherrill died in 2014.

Representative Works

The Accidental President, 1967.

Gothic Politics in the Deep South: Stars of the New Confederacy, 1968, revised 1969, revised 1991.

Military Justice Is to Justice as Military Music Is to Music, 1970.

Why They Call It Politics: A Guide to America's Government, 1972.

The Saturday Night Special, and Other Guns with Which Americans Won the West, Protected Bootleg Franchises, Slew Wildlife, Robbed Countless Banks, Shot Husbands Purposely and by Mistake, and Killed Presidents, 1973.

The Last Kennedy: Edward M. Kennedy of Massachusetts, Before and After Chappaquiddick, 1976.

The Oil Follies of 1970–1980: How the Petroleum Industry Stole the Show (And Much More Besides), 1983.

Further Reading

Ivins, Molly. "Robert Sherrill: Journalism His Way." *Washington Journalism Review* 7.11(Nov. 1985).

Navasky, Victor. "Robert Sherrill, 1924–2014." *The Nation* 299.11 (15 Sept. 2014).

Robert Sherrill. *Gale Literature: Contemporary Authors*. Detroit: Gale, 2014.

Yardley, William. "Robert Sherrill, Author Who Skewered Right and Left, Dies at 89." *The New York Times* (22 Aug 2014).

James B. Steele, Jr. (1943–)

James B. Steele was born on January 3, 1943, in Hutchinson, Kansas, and was educated at the University of Missouri at Kansas City, from which he graduated in 1967.

Steele worked as a reporter at *The Kansas City Times* from 1962 to 1967. He moved to Washington, D. C., in 1968 and worked as the director of information for the Laborers' International Union of North America.

In 1970 he was hired as an investigative journalist by *The Philadelphia Inquirer*, where he teamed up with Donald L. Barlett who had been hired the same year. With Barlett, Steele wrote numerous investigative articles about various topics for the newspaper. Generally, these articles focused on an office or bureau of the local, state, or federal government. In fact, he and Barlett received various awards for their stories or series over the years. Several of their lengthy articles were expanded and published as pamphlets and books, including *Oil: The Created Crisis*, which was published in 1973; *Empire: The Life, Legend, and Madness of Howard Hughes*, which was published in 1979; *Forevermore: Nuclear Waste in America*, which was published in 1985; *America: What Went Wrong?*, which was published in 1992; *America: Who Really Pays the Taxes?*, which was published in 1994; *America: Who Stole the Dream?*, which was published in 1996; *The Great America Tax Dodge: How Spiraling Fraud and Avoidance Are Killing Fairness, Destroying the Income Tax, and Costing You*, which was published in 2000; *Critical Condition: How Health Care in America Became Big Business—and Bad Medicine*, which was published in 2004; *The Betrayal of the American Dream*, which was published in 2012; and *America: What Went Wrong?: The Crisis Deepens*, which was published in 2020.

One of their first series of articles for the newspaper concerned fraud in the Federal Housing Administration's subsidy program. In order to do this series well, they employed computers to search numerous records. In fact, they used computers to gather information for numerous topics.

Generally, they searched through records to verify facts. They did not necessarily rely on what informants had provided. They relied on data to support what had been told to them.

Although articles about other subjects followed, the journalists were not pressured by any editor to have any article written by such and such time or day. They were allowed to investigate whatever interested them.

Steele and Barlett left *The Philadelphia Inquirer* in 1997 and moved to *Time*, where they stayed for several years. They moved to *Vanity Fair* in 2007.

Representative Works

Oil: The Created Crisis (with Donald L. Barlett), 1973.
Empire: The Life, Legend, and Madness of Howard Hughes (with Donald L. Barlett), 1979.
Forevermore: Nuclear Waste in America (with Donald L. Barlett), 1985.
America: What Went Wrong? (with Donald L. Barlett), 1992.
America: Who Really Pays the Taxes? (with Donald L. Barlett), 1994.
America: Who Stole the Dream? (with Donald L. Barlett), 1996.
The Great America Tax Dodge: How Spiraling Fraud and Avoidance Are Killing Fairness, Destroying the Income Tax, and Costing You (with Donald L. Barlett), 2000.
Critical Condition: How Health Care in America Became Big Business—and Bad Medicine (with Donald L. Barlett), 2004.
The Betrayal of the American Dream (with Donald L. Barlett), 2012.
America: What Went Wrong?: The Crisis Deepens (with Donald L. Barlett), 2020.

Further Reading

Downie, Leonard, Jr. *The New Muckrakers*. New York: New Republic, 1976.
Dygert, James H. *The Investigative Journalist: Folk Heroes of a New Era.* New York: Prentice-Hall, 1976.
Weinberg, Steve. "In Defense of 'Expert Journalism,'" *Columbia Journalism Review* (Jan. –Feb. 1997).

Herbert Bayard Swope (1882–1958)

Born on January 5, 1882, in St. Louis, Missouri, to Ida Cohn and Isaac Swope, who had emigrated from Germany to the United States, Herbert Bayard Swope had an older brother and two older sisters. Mischievous as a child, Swope was expelled when he was a freshman in high school. Fortunately, he was readmitted and eventually graduated.

Unfortunately, Swope's father died before 1900. His mother and sisters moved to Germany, where they stayed most of the time for the remainder of their lives. Swope's older brother, Gerard, had studied electronics at the Massachusetts Institute of Technology and was working in Chicago. Swope went with his mother and sisters and toured Germany. He attended lectures at a university, but he was not studious like Gerard. Consequently, when he returned to the United States, he was not interested in attending college.

Instead, Swope worked in an electrical shop in Chicago, but he hated the job so much that he quit and returned to St. Louis. He found different jobs, but none excited him. Finally, in 1900, a friend helped him get a job as a reporter at *The St. Louis Post-Dispatch*. Swope enjoyed visiting the race track during working hours and was fired. He returned to Chicago and got a job as a reporter at *The Chicago Inter-Ocean*, another newspaper. However, he did not stay long at the paper or in Chicago.

In 1901 he was recruited to work as a reporter for *The New York Herald*. Swope was young and the atmosphere of New York City appealed to him. He met John Barrymore who worked as a cartoonist for *The New York Morning Telegraph* and later *The New York Evening Journal* before Barrymore became a successful actor. In fact, the two became good friends.

Swope was fired in 1903 primarily because he would not necessarily show up to work and because he seldom wrote about what had been assigned to him. Although he enjoyed journalism, he was not a very responsible reporter. He wondered what he would do next.

In the few years he had been in New York City, Swope had grown to enjoy the many restaurants, the various theaters, and horse racing. However, he needed a job. Soon, he found work as a press agent for a touring theater group. Although this position allowed him to meet professional actors, he missed journalism.

He gave up being a press agent when he became a reporter for *The New York Morning Telegraph*. However, he did not necessarily like the job or the newspaper. Consequently, in 1904 he approached the editor at *The New York*

Herald, who agreed to hire him again. One of his assignments was to cover Prince Louis of Battenberg (later Mountbatten), an admiral in the British navy. Of course, he covered other subjects as well, but it was not long before his old habits interfered with his work. He was fired again in 1907.

About a year later he met Margaret Honeyman Powell, the woman he would marry in 1912 and live with until his death.

Swope, along with another former reporter, worked in public relations, but this job did not last long primarily because there were too few clients.

In 1909 Swope landed a job as a reporter for *The New York World*, which was owned by Joseph Pulitzer. According to Swope, Pulitzer was one of the four best newspaper publishers in the country. Swope wrote primarily investigative articles. In 1912 he traveled to Nova Scotia to interview the survivors of the *Titanic*, which had hit an iceberg, causing it to sink. In 1913 and 1914 he wrote an expose about the police being involved in the murder of Herman Rosenthal, a gambler, who had agreed to talk to the district attorney about how the police were protecting big-time gamblers. Swope wrote the stories pertaining to Rosenthal's murder, the police officers who were responsible, their convictions, and their sentences. He even helped track down the suspects.

In 1914, during World War I, Swope journeyed to Germany, where he wrote about the sinking of three British warships by a German submarine and about the German military forces entering Belgium, among other stories. When he returned to the United States, he was promoted to city editor.

He returned to Germany in 1916 and wrote more stories about the war. Eventually, his articles made up the book *Inside the German Empire in the Third Year of the War*, which was published in 1917. Swope received a Pulitzer Prize the same year.

Swope was sent to Washington, D.C., to learn about the conduct of the war. Bernard Baruch, the head of the War Industries Board, met Swope and the two became friends. In fact, Swope agreed to work briefly for the Board.

After the war, in 1918, Swope went to Paris, where he wrote about the Versailles Peace Conference. Although he supported President Woodrow Wilson's plans for Europe, he grew disillusioned when the governments of the United States and other countries compromised.

After he learned about his wife suffering a nervous breakdown, he returned to the United States and tended to her welfare. When he returned to *The New York World*, he was promoted to executive editor. He held the position from 1920 to 1928. Swope favored crusades about various subjects, including the Ku Klux Klan and the so-called League of Nations. He personally took an interest in the new Op-Ed page. Indeed, he solicited well-known writers such as Heywood Broun to contribute columns or other material to it. Swope helped make the paper one of the best in New York City at the time.

Concurrently, as executive editor, he realized he needed to become involved in politics to a certain extent. He helped bring the Democratic Convention to New York City in 1924. Generally, politics and politicians were only interesting to Swope because both were interesting to readers of the newspaper. However, during the next presidential election, he strongly supported Alfred E. Smith, the Democratic candidate for president, because he thought Smith was the most intelligent person running. When Smith was defeated, Swope took his defeat personally.

In 1928 Swope resigned from his position at the paper, much to the chagrin of the publisher. He served his community and helped politicians in government. He served on several boards and entertained well-known guests at his estate in Sands Point, New York. He played high-stakes poker and enjoyed croquet.

Several years later, when *The New York World* was being sold, he tried to raise enough money to purchase it, but he was not successful.

When gambling on horse racing became legal in New York, he served as the chairman of the New York Racing Commission from 1934 to 1945.

During World War II, he served as a civilian advisor, for which he received a Medal of Merit in 1947.

He died on June 20, 1958, of pneumonia at his estate.

Representative Work

Inside the German Empire in the Third Year of the War, 1917.

Further Reading

Baruch, Bernard M. *My Own Story*. New York: Holt, 1957.

Baruch, Bernard M. *The Public Years*. New York: Holt, Rinehart & Winston, 1960.

"Death of a Reporter." *Time* (30 June 1958).

Kahn, E. J. *The World of Swope*. New York: Simon & Schuster, 1965.

Lewis, Alfred Allan. *Man of the World; Herbert Bayard Swope: A Charmed Life of Pulitzer Prizes, Poker and Politics*. Indianapolis: Bobbs-Merrill, 1978.

"Swope of the World." *Newsweek* (30 June 1958).

Eva McDonald Valesh ("Eva Gay") (1866–1956)

Eva Valesh used the pseudonym "Eva Gay" when she wrote investigative articles about women who worked outside the home for the *St. Paul Daily Globe*.

Valesh was born on September 9, 1866, in Orono, Maine. Her parents, John and Elinor Lane McDonald, had immigrated to the United States. The family moved to Minnesota several years later, before Eva entered the high school in Minneapolis. She graduated when she was fifteen years of age.

Although Eva studied to be a teacher, she could not find a job probably because of her age. She turned to journalism and contributed articles to the *Saturday Evening Spectator*. However, she was not paid very much. She trained to be a typesetter and joined the union for typographers. (In fact, later, activism for unions, particularly for unions that helped women, would become personal to her.)

She continued to write journalism, however, and, at the urging of the editor of the *St. Paul Daily Globe*, she started writing investigative articles under the pseudonym "Eva Gay" about young women who worked in factories in Minneapolis. Valesh interviewed young women who worked in various factories and described the poor conditions in which they toiled. She pointed out that their salaries were based on the number of pieces produced, not necessarily the time the young women spent producing each piece. She also mentioned that their salaries had been decreased, not increased, during the past year.

These factories were not called "sweatshops" at the time, but they certainly could have been because of the conditions Valesh described.

After one or two articles appeared, female workers at a garment factory went on strike because of a decrease in salary. Even though Valesh's articles were mentioned as inspiring the strike, the Knights of Labor, an organization that represented workers, actually organized the strike. Representatives of the factory provided several compromises, including a higher salary to new employees, but they would not guarantee that each woman who went on strike could have her job back. Eventually, the factory closed.

Eva wrote another investigative article about working conditions in several laundries, which she found to be very poor. She mentioned that the washroom, for instance, was steamy primarily because of poor ventilation. The female workers averaged twelve hours a day, not ten, which management had claimed was the maximum number of hours each woman worked. Eva pointed out that even though a bonus could be earned, seldom did a female worker last long enough at her job to earn it.

Like Nell Nelson in Chicago, Gay found jobs and reported about what she observed and experienced. She interviewed others and reported what they said. Overall, she found working conditions horrible.

Gay continued her series of stories for more than a year. As a result of her popularity and professional skills, she was promoted to editor of the labor section and, later, worked at *The Minneapolis Daily Tribune*.

In 1891 she married Frank S. Valesh. They had helped found the Minnesota State Federation of Labor in 1890. Frank served as the assistant commissioner of labor, but his health deteriorated so he retired. Eventually, he oversaw a small factory that made cigars in Graceville, Minnesota.

In 1895 Eva traveled to Europe and wrote about working conditions for women. These articles were published in *The American Federationist*, a publication of the American Federation of Labor, a union that represented workers.

As if traveling and writing were not enough, Eva worked as a speaker and organizer for the Knights of Labor and the Eight Hour League. Ignatius Donnelly, the president of the Minnesota Farmers' Alliance, grew impressed with Eva's writing and speaking ability that he appealed to her to become a speaker for the Farmers' Alliance, which she did.

Eva and Frank separated in the late 1890s and finally divorced in 1906.

Eva left Minnesota and moved to New York City, where she worked as a reporter for *The New York Journal American*. She wrote about several different subjects, including crime, politics, strikes, and war in Cuba. Later, after she had left the newspaper, she co-wrote a sheet about politics, which was syndicated to magazines and newspapers.

Samuel Gompers, the president of the American Federation of Labor, encouraged her to become the assistant editor of the union's magazine, *The American Federationist*. As the assistant editor, she wrote about women and children who worked outside the home as well as education for the publication. Unfortunately, much of her work was published under "Gompers" name, not hers.

In 1911 Eva founded the *American Club Woman*, a magazine. She edited the monthly that promoted conservative activism and other subjects that were popular to women at the time until 1920.

Eva married Benjamin Cross, but their marriage ended in 1923. For the next few decades, Eva proofread copy at *The New York Times*.

She died in 1956.

Representative Works

"Mong Girls Who Toil," *St. Paul Daily Globe*, March 25, 1888.
"The Toiling Women," *St. Paul Daily Globe*, April 1, 1888.
"Song of the Shirt," *St. Paul Daily Globe*, April 8, 1888.
"Working in the Wet," *St. Paul Daily Globe*, April 15, 1888.
"Striking Maidens," *St. Paul Daily Globe*, April 29, 1888.
"Girls Make Money," *St. Paul Daily Globe*, May 13, 1888.
"Workers in Wool," *St. Paul Daily Globe*, May 20, 1888.
"Girls Make Cigars," *St. Paul Daily Globe*, May 27, 1888.
"Girls Make Boxes," *St. Paul Daily Globe*, June 3, 1888.
"The Sewing Girls," *St. Paul Daily Globe*, June 10, 1888.
"How Girls Clerk," *St. Paul Daily Globe*, June 17, 1888.
"In Cap and Apron," *St. Paul Daily Globe*, July 15, 1888.
"Girls in Politics," *St. Paul Daily Globe*, August 19, 1888.
"Who Keeps the Cash," *St. Paul Daily Globe*, September 2, 1888.
"Shorthand Fever," *St. Paul Daily Globe*, September 23, 1888.
"Yes, You Know Her," *St. Paul Daily Globe*, November 4, 1888.
"Didn't Fill the Bill," *St. Paul Daily Globe*, December 2, 1888.
"Makes Girls Blind," *St. Paul Daily Globe*, December 25, 1888.
"Dress Reform Craze," *St. Paul Daily Globe*, February 17, 1889.
"And So She Flunked," *St. Paul Daily Globe*, February 24, 1889.
"Like Birds of Prey," *St. Paul Daily Globe*, March 3, 1889.
"Catches the Ladies," *St. Paul Daily Globe*, March 19, 1889.

Further Reading

Faue, Elizabeth. *Writing the Wrongs: Eva Valesh and the Rise of Labor Journalism*. Ithaca, N. Y.: Cornell University Press, 2002.

Gilman, Rhoda R. "Eva McDonald Valesh, Minnesota Populist." *Women of Minnesota: Selected Biographical Essays*. Ed. Barbara Stuhler and Gretchen Kreuter. St. Paul: Minnesota Historical Society Press, 1977.

Gary Webb (1955–2004)

Gary Webb was born on August 31, 1955, to Anita and William Webb, in Corona, California. He attended Indiana University-Purdue University in Indianapolis in the early 1970s and then Northern Kentucky University from the mid- to late-1970s. However, he did not earn a degree.

Webb worked as a journalist for the *News Journal* in Carmel, Indiana, for at least a year in the mid-1970s. From the late 1970s to the early 1980s he worked as an investigative journalist for the *Kentucky Post* in Covington. He wrote about political corruption and the coal industry. He moved to the *Cleveland Plain Dealer* in 1983 and worked as an investigative journalist covering the government. In 1988 he moved to the *San Jose Mercury News*, for which he worked as an investigative journalist in Sacramento. In 1996 he contributed a four-part series about the Central Intelligence Agency (CIA) and its ties to drug cartels to his editor. After several confrontations about the series with the editor, including its length, the series was cut to three parts.

Later, after the series had appeared in print and on the web, several reporters and editors at larger metropolitan dailies started asking questions about Webb's allegations. Had the CIA encouraged one of the major drug cartels to bring cocaine into the United States and sell it in depressed neighborhoods? Had the profits from the sales been used to support the Contras, the militants that had attempted to overthrow the socialist government in Nicaragua?

Although Webb had received numerous awards for his investigative journalism over the years, his series about the CIA was eventually criticized by other reporters and editors, not to mention government officials. In fact, as Jeff Leen pointed out, "*The New York Times*, *The Washington Post*, and the *Los Angeles Times* ... all wrote major pieces knocking the story down for its overblown claims and undernourished reporting."[1]

The *San Jose Mercury News* later apologized for the series. Although Webb was not fired, he was no longer given major assignments. Consequently, he left the newspaper a year later.

Webb worked as a consultant to the state legislature in Sacramento. Specifically, he became a researcher for the Joint Legislative Audit Committee, which investigated the governor's questionable decisions regarding bidding contracts, among other issues.

1 Jeff Leen, "Gary Webb Was No Journalism Hero, Despite What 'Kill the Messenger' Says." *The Washington Post*, October 17, 2014.

Webb wrote *Dark Alliance: The CIA, the Contras, and the Crack Cocaine Explosion*, which was based on his series that had appeared in the newspaper as well as other information. The book was published in 1998.

The series as well as the book led to investigations by the CIA and the Department of Justice.

According to officials, Webb died of two self-inflicted gunshot wounds on December 9, 2004. He was forty-nine years old.

Representative Work

Dark Alliance: The CIA, the Contras, and the Crack Cocaine Explosion, 1998.

Further Reading

Carr, David. "Resurrecting a Disgraced Reporter." *The New York Times*, October 5, 2014.

Gary, Webb. *Gale Literature: Contemporary Authors*. Detroit: Gale, 2008.

Paterno, Susan. "The Sad Saga of Gary Webb." *American Journalism Review* (June–July 2005).

Schou, Nick. *Kill the Messenger: How the CIA's Crack-Cocaine Controversy Destroyed Journalist Gary Webb*. New York: Bold Type Books, 2009.

Ida B. Wells-Barnett ("Iola") (1862–1931)

Ida B. Wells was born on July 16, 1862, to Elizabeth or "Lizzie" and Jim Wells, in Holly Springs, Mississippi. In 1878 her youngest brother and parents died from yellow fever. Ida was only sixteen and was enrolled in high school classes at Shaw University, which later became Rust College.

Since she was the oldest child, she realized she had to find a job so she could take care of her siblings. She styled her hair on top of her head into a bun to make herself appear older. Then she found a job as a teacher in Holly Springs. Her two oldest brothers found jobs in Holly Springs and moved out.

In order to earn more for her and her remaining siblings, Ida moved to Memphis, where she taught at a school for African Americans. She earned a few dollars more than she earned in Holly Springs. However, she realized she needed to earn more. During the summer she attended Fisk University in Nashville, Tennessee, and wrote articles for the student newspaper. She enjoyed journalism, but she realized few women—especially African-American women—worked in this profession. Besides, even white women who worked in journalism did not earn as much as their male counterparts.

When the *Evening Star*, a religious literary publication, needed an editor, Ida volunteered. Of course, she kept her job as a teacher, too, primarily because the publication did not pay much, if anything.

As a result of her experience in journalism, she became the editor of *The Living Way*, a small newspaper. Even though she was the editor, she contributed editorials and other matter to this publication as well as to the other. She used the pseudonym "Iola." Most of her contributions concerned problems African Americans experienced at the time. Indeed, Iola sought equal justice under the law for African Americans.

In 1884, while sitting in a first-class railroad car with other women, Ida was told by the conductor that she was sitting in a car for "whites only" and that she would have to move to the smoking car. Ida refused because she had purchased a first-class ticket. She and the conductor argued until several men removed her from the car. Soon after, she got off the train.

Later, Ida sued the Chesapeake, Ohio and Southwestern Railroad and won, but a few years later the Tennessee Supreme Court overturned the lower court's ruling. Although she had eventually lost her suit, she had exhibited a willingness to confront the establishment. Such action was rare in the late 1800s, especially by African Americans.

In an article that appeared in *The Living Way* in 1887, she explained in detail the reason for her lawsuit against the railroad. The article was printed in other newspapers that were read by African Americans. As a result, several editors of these newspapers asked her to submit articles to their newspapers, which she did.

Ida's reputation as an editor and journalist spread among editors and journalists who worked at newspapers read by African Americans. Soon, the owners of the *Memphis Free Speech and Headlight*, a small weekly newspaper, invited her to join their paper. Ida insisted she be allowed to invest in the publication, serve as editor and sales manager, and keep her job as a teacher. The owners agreed.

At the time, Ida was unlike most African-American women. Indeed, few could read and write, let alone work as an editor and sales manager of a newspaper. Yet, Ida became an example for other African-American women to emulate. She proved African-American women could do whatever African-American men could do, perhaps more, especially if they felt compelled.

In addition to serving as editor and sales manager, Ida contributed regularly to the paper. Unfortunately, in one of her editorials, she criticized the school board in Memphis for not supporting education for African Americans. As a result, she lost her job as a teacher.

Now, Ida was forced to concentrate solely on the newspaper. In order to boost circulation and earn more, she traveled through various counties in Mississippi, Arkansas, and Tennessee. She persuaded African Americans to not only read the newspaper but become subscribers to it. Within months her travels paid off. The newspaper's circulation increased. Ida's income was almost as much as it was when she was teaching.

In her contributions to the paper she criticized African Americans for taking advantage of other African Americans. She complained about African Americans being incarcerated for minor crimes when whites were not. She criticized the federal government for not protecting African Americans in the South.

In Memphis a few African-American businessmen opened a grocery store near another grocery store that was owned by a white businessman. In 1892, apparently after the white businessman realized his former patrons were shopping at the other store, he encouraged whites to cause trouble, which they did. They burned the grocery store that was owned by the African Americans and, later, lynched them. Outraged, Ida encouraged African Americans to boycott every business owned by a white person in Memphis. Then she called on African Americans to move away from Memphis. Over several years about two thousand moved to other towns and cities.

In addition, Ida started investigating lynching and eventually determined that its purpose was to stop African Americans from succeeding. She also believed its purpose was to stop African Americans from thinking they were equal to whites. Of course, she acknowledged that "rape" claimed by white women had been used often as a justification for lynching an African-American man, but she learned that "rape" had not been claimed in most cases.

As a result of her articles, numerous whites went to the office of the *Memphis Free Speech and Headlight* and destroyed it. Fortunately, Ida was traveling at the time and was not harmed. However, she immediately realized she would not be safe in Memphis. She had to move away.

Ida went to New York, where T. Thomas Fortune was publishing the *New York Age*. Fortune offered Ida part of the newspaper in return for the list of subscribers to the *Memphis Free Speech and Headlight*, which she accepted.

Ida continued her crusade against lynching. For instance, the newspaper included her lengthy article about what had happened in Memphis. However, Ida was not finished. In article after article she revealed the history of lynching in the South, the number of hangings for a certain period, and other factual information. She even included data from other sources, such as *The Chicago Tribune*. In addition to her articles, she wrote the pamphlet *Southern Horrors: Lynch Law in All Its Phases*, which was published in 1892.

Ida became well-known and was invited to speak about the subject by various groups in New York and elsewhere in New England. Of course, Ida hoped northerners would join her in her cause and would put pressure on various politicians who served in the United States Congress. Without question she hoped the United States Congress would enact legislation that would end lynching in the South. However, her hopes were dashed when she realized that many northerners felt they were powerless to do anything or, worse, were not concerned whatsoever. After all, lynching was a problem in the South, not in the North.

In 1893 she was invited to tour and speak about the subject in Great Britain. Ida accepted. Her words appeared in several newspapers in Great Britain before she ended her tour.

Upon her return she settled in Chicago. With Frederick Douglass, Ferdinand Barnett, and I. Garland Penn, she co-wrote the pamphlet *The Reason Why the Colored American Is Not in the World's Columbian Exposition*, which was published in 1893 and circulated at the world's fair in Chicago. She also wrote for the *Chicago Conservator*, a small newspaper that was founded and edited by Ferdinand Barnett, an attorney, and later for the *Chicago Inter-Ocean*, a large newspaper. Both newspapers were well-known and respected.

Ida was invited to tour and speak in Great Britain again in 1894. She accepted and contributed articles about her experiences abroad to the *Chicago Inter-Ocean*. Ida remained in Great Britain several months before she returned to Chicago.

In 1895 Ida wrote another pamphlet about lynching. Titled *A Red Record: Tabulated Statistics and Alleged Causes of Lynching in the United States, 1892-1893-1894*, the pamphlet, which was published the same year, contained more information about lynching in the United States. In fact, it included the number of African-American men who had been murdered in the South for the years mentioned in the title.

The same year Ida married Ferdinand Barnett. Soon after the marriage, Ida became the editor of the newspaper while Ferdinand focused on law. She had one child and then another. Eventually, she had four children. She accepted motherhood extremely well. She decreased her obligations outside the home until her children started school. Then she grew interested in organizations that were for African-American women. Later, she put her energies in political causes, including the women's suffrage movement.

Although she and her husband sold the newspaper, Ida was still interested in writing articles and pamphlets about lynching. For instance, in 1900 she wrote the pamphlet *Mob Rule in New Orleans: Robert Charles and His Fight to the Death*, which was published the same year. Ida presented factual information along with her opinions about lynching.

In 1909 she traveled to southern Illinois to investigate the lynching of an African-American man. Ida learned the sheriff could have tried to prevent it from occurring, but he had not taken any action. Her article about the incident appeared in the *Chicago Defender* in 1910.

She investigated the race riots in East St. Louis, Illinois, for the *Chicago Defender* in 1918. She investigated the race riots in Little Rock, Arkansas, in 1922. Ida learned the riots had been a reaction to several farmers being charged for murder. Her report *The Arkansas Race Riot* was published in 1922.

Ida started writing her autobiography in 1928, when she was in her sixties. She recounted her struggles, her disagreements with other African Americans, her anti-lynching crusade, and her life. Although she never completed it, what she had written was published posthumously under the title *Crusade for Justice: The Autobiography of Ida B. Wells* in 1970.

Ida died on March 25, 1931.

Representative Work

Southern Horrors: Lynch Law in All Its Phases, 1892.

The Reason Why the Colored American is Not in the World's Columbian Exposition (with Frederick Douglass, Ferdinand L. Barnett, and I. Garland Penn), 1893.

A Red Record: Tabulated Statistics and Alleged Causes of Lynching in the United States, 1892-1893-1894, 1895.

Mob Rule in New Orleans: Robert Charles and His Fight to the Death, 1900.

"Lynch Law in America." *Arena*, 23, January 1900.

"Lynching An Excuse for it." *The Independent*, 53, May 1901.

"How Enfranchisement Stops Lynchings." *Original Rights Magazine*, 2, June 1910.

"Our Country's Lynching Record." *Survey*, 29, February 1913.

Crusade for Justice: The Autobiography of Ida B. Wells, 1970.

Further Reading

Duster, Alfreda M., ed. *Crusade for Justice: The Autobiography of Ida B. Wells*. Chicago: University of Chicago Press, 1970.

Giddings, Paula J. *Ida: A Sword Among Lions: Ida B. Wells and the Campaign Against Lynching*. New York: Harper Collins Publishers, 2009.

McMurry, Linda O. *To Keep the Waters Troubled: The Life of Ida B. Wells*. New York: Oxford University Press, 1999.

Sterling, Dorothy. *Black Foremothers: Three Lives*. Old Westbury, New York: Feminist Press, 1979.

Thompson, Mildred I. *Ida B. Wells-Barnett: An Exploratory Study of an American Black Woman, 1893–1930*. Brooklyn, New York: Carlson Publishing, 1990.

Tucker, David M. "Miss Ida B. Wells and Memphis Lynching." *Phylon* 32 (Summer 1971).

Duff Wilson (1954–)

Duff Wilson was born in 1954, in the state of Washington, where his parents owned a small-town newspaper, the *Omak Chronicle*. Wilson actually started his career in journalism when he was in his early teens, working at his parents' newspaper.

He attended Western Washington University, from which he graduated in 1976, and the Graduate School of Journalism at Columbia University, from which he graduated in 1982.

Wilson worked for the Associated Press (AP) before he became a reporter for the *Seattle Post-Intelligencer* in 1982. Seven years later he moved to *The Seattle Times*. In 1992 he wrote about Democrat Brock Adams, a United States Senator who had sexually abused a congressional aide.

A few years later Wilson and Eric Nalder, another journalist, wrote about the Martin Pang Warehouse fire. They wrote about the arsonist, whom they had uncovered, as well as about the several mistakes members of the fire department made. Unfortunately, these mistakes led to the deaths of four firefighters.

One of Wilson's major investigative series was "Fear in the Fields," which exposed the use of hazardous material in making fertilizers that were used by farmers throughout the country. The idea for the series and later the book *Fateful Harvest: The True Story of a Small Town, a Global Industry, and a Toxic Secret*, which was published in 2001, was sparked by Patty Martin, who was mayor of Quincy, Washington, at the time. She informed Wilson that something in her community was making people and animals sick. She believed the problem was the fertilizer being used in the area.

Wilson investigated and learned that industries were allowed to recycle byproducts that were produced during the production of products the industries sold. These products, including chemicals and even radioactive materials, could end up in fertilizers that farmers used.

After the series and book were published, a few states, including Washington, actually enacted legislation that restricted how byproducts were used in fertilizers. Even the Environmental Protection Agency looked at the issue.

In 2001 Wilson and David Heath wrote the five-part series "Uninformed Consent: What patients at 'The Hutch' weren't told about the experiment in which they died." The series concerned clinical trials at the Fred Hutchinson Cancer Research Center in Seattle. According to the journalists' reports, the patients died prematurely because of the trials. However, the patients and their families had not been informed about the risks. Nor had they been informed about the doctors conducting the trials.

Wilson left *The Seattle Times* in 2004 for *The New York Times*. He wrote about the members of Duke University's lacrosse team being accused of raping a woman. He wrote about athletes using steroids. He also wrote about various drugs and pharmaceutical companies.

He left *The New York Times* in 2012 and became an adjunct faculty member in the Graduate School of Journalism at Columbia University as well as an investigative reporter and associate editor for Reuters.

Wilson and John Shiffman co-wrote the three-part series "Helpless and Hooked" in 2015 for Reuters. The journalists examined thousands of pages of documents and interviewed several hundred people about the effects of opioids on newborn infants.

The series concerned the failures of the Child Abuse Prevention and Treatment Act, which had been amended to make certain hospitals notify Child Protective Services about any infant that was born with an addiction to drugs. The series revealed that hospitals had failed to report every newborn with a problem and that Child Protection Services had failed to protect the infants about which they had been informed. As a result, more than 100 babies had died needlessly.

In addition to teaching and writing investigative journalism, Wilson has developed materials for the organization "Investigative Reporters and Editors."

Representative Works

"Fear in the Fields," 1997.

Fateful Harvest: The True Story of a Small Town, a Global Industry, and a Toxic Secret, 2001.

"Uninformed Consent: What patients at 'The Hutch' weren't told about the experiment in Which they died," 2001.

"Helpless and Hooked" (with John Sheffman), 2015.

Further Reading

Anderson, Kurt, "The Imperial City: Rape, Justice, and the 'Times: "I've never felt so Ill." *New York* (16 Oct. 2006).

Duff Wilson. *The Writer's Directory*. Detroit: St. James Press, 2018.

Duff Wilson. *Columbia Journalism Review* 40.1 (May–June 2002).

Duff Wilson. *Gale Literature: Contemporary Authors*. Detroit: Gale, 2002.

Suberchicot, Alain. "On Duff Wilson: Community, Agribusiness and Environmental Testimony." *Environmental Awareness and the Design of Literature*. Ed. Francois Specq. Boston, MA: Brill Academic Publisher, 2017.

David Wise (1930–2018)

David Wise was born in New York City on May 10, 1930, and was educated at Columbia University, from which he graduated in 1951. He worked for *The New York Herald Tribune* in various capacities, including reporter, White House correspondent, and chief of the Washington bureau, from 1951 to 1966.

Principally a political reporter and investigator, Wise, with Thomas B. Ross, wrote *The U-2 Affair* in 1962, when interest in the Francis Gary Powers' spy mission was at its zenith. The authors collaborated on another investigative book two years later. Titled *The Invisible Government*, the book included several important revelations about the political machine in Washington, D. C. For example, Wise and Ross disclosed that Richard Nixon had wanted the Cuban invasion to take place before the 1960 election. Furthermore, the authors examined the special group "54/12," which, at the discretion of the president, had the power to rule on certain clandestine operations without the approval of Congress.

Wise and Ross wrote another intriguing book entitled *The Espionage Establishment*, which was published in 1967. The authors attempted to prove the validity of two controversial theories regarding the Central Intelligence Agency (CIA): (1) the organization was not responsible to or controllable by any political body except itself and (2) the organization engaged in domestic operations.

Without the aid of Ross, Wise wrote the disturbing and revealing book *The Politics of Lying: Government Deception, Secrecy and Power*, which was published in 1973. Wise recapitulated what he and Ross had mentioned in previous books and then attacked the Wartime Information Security Program, the federal government's dubious role in the Dominican Republic and South Vietnam, and the press's failure to investigate and report the lies perpetrated by political leaders and agencies.

In addition to books about political intrigue, Wise contributed articles of a similar nature to magazines.

He wrote another in-depth political expose in 1976. Titled *The American Police State: The Government Against the People*, the author discussed the numerous manipulations by the Nixon administration. Without question the book illustrated the author's direct approach to the subject matter.

Wise wrote the penetrating book *The Spy Who Got Away: The Inside Story of Edward Lee Howard, the CIA Agent Who Betrayed His Country's Secrets and Escaped to Moscow*. Published in 1988, the book told the incredible story of the first CIA defector to the former Soviet Union. Wise had interviewed ex-CIA agent Edward Lee Howard in 1987, two years after his defection, and combined the information he had obtained from Howard with other information he had collected over the years and revealed what had been a confusing chain of events. Indeed, Wise told how Howard destroyed the United States' espionage network in the former Soviet Union, how he was fired from the CIA, how he was placed under surveillance by the FBI, how he managed to escape to Moscow, and how he betrayed the CIA by exposing certain secrets to the former Soviet Union's KGB. The book was riveting, to say the least, primarily because it contained the elements usually found in a suspense novel.

Four years later his book *Molehunt: The Secret Search for Traitors That Shattered the CIA* was published. Wise revealed that the search for spies inside the CIA actually destroyed the careers of some loyal officers as well as the lives of certain members of their families. The agency was also paralyzed by the search. For instance, the agency halted its operations against the former Soviet Union during the height of the Cold War. The author's narrative was as absorbing as it was carefully researched. The book was based on more than 600 interviews with more than 200 individuals.

Wise wrote *Nightmover: How Aldrich Ames Sold the CIA to the KGB for $4.6 Million*, which was published in 1995. In this book Wise told about Aldrich Ames who enjoyed alcohol, women, and money. Although Ames was not necessarily good at his job, eventually he was placed in a position that allowed him to gather information that was valuable to agents who worked for the former Soviet Union. As a result, several agents of the United States who operated in Moscow were killed. Finally, in 1986, a group was formed inside the agency to learn who the mole or moles were. After several years, the mole was identified, and the FBI was asked to investigate him and his wife. In 1994 Ames and his wife were arrested.

Cassidy's Run: The Secret Spy War Over Nerve Gas was published in 2000. Wise explored "Operation Shocker," an espionage operation initiated by the FBI against the former Soviet Union during the early years of the Cold War. Wise focused on Sergeant Joe Cassidy. Cassidy, who was in the military, was not trained as a spy; yet, he became one for the FBI and passed mostly so-called secret formulas to agents of the former Soviet Union. Unfortunately, one of these formulas, which was considered to be unusable, may have helped the former Soviet Union to develop a revolutionary nerve gas.

In 2002 Wise's *Spy: The Inside Story of How the FBI's Robert Hanssen Betrayed America* was published. In this book Wise revealed how Robert

Hanssen, who worked for the FBI, sold secrets to agents of the former Soviet Union for almost twenty-two years before he was arrested. As Wise pointed out, Hanssen had betrayed himself, his family, his friends, his employer, and his country.

Tiger Trap: America's Secret Spy War with China was published in 2011. Wise interviewed more than 150 people for this book and learned that the country's intelligence efforts may have been focused too much on the former Soviet Union and not enough on Communist China. Wise learned that Communist China generally recruited individuals who did not have psychological or emotional problems. In fact, China typically recruited Americans who were from China or were of Chinese descent. If recruited, these individuals generally were asked to steal information about nuclear weapons in the United States or penetrate the country's counterintelligence activities. Wise explored several cases, including Katrina Leung, who was called Parlor Maid and who operated as a double agent for the FBI and Communist China's Ministry of State Security (MSS). Tiger Trap referred to the operation that exposed the Chinese-American scientist who was suspected of stealing secrets from one of the nuclear weapons laboratories in the United States.

In addition to his nonfiction books, Wise wrote about espionage in at least three novels: *Spectrum*, which was published in 1981; *The Children's Game*, which was published in 1983; and *The Samarkand Dimension*, which was published in 1987.

Wise died in 2018. He was 88 years old.

Representative Works

The U-2 Affair (with Thomas B. Ross), 1962.
The Invisible Government (with Thomas B. Ross), 1964.
The Espionage Establishment (with Thomas B. Ross), 1967.
The Politics of Lying: Government Deception, Secrecy and Power, 1973.
The American Police State: The Government Against the People, 1976.
The Spy Who Got Away: The Inside Story of Edward Lee Howard, the CIA Agent Who Betrayed His Country's Secrets and Escaped to Moscow, 1988.
Molehunt: The Secret Search for Traitors That Shattered the CIA, 1992.
Nightmover: How Aldrich Ames Sold the CIA to the KGB for $4.6 Million, 1995.
Cassidy's Run: The Secret Spy War Over Nerve Gas, 2000.
Spy: The Inside Story of How the FBI's Robert Hanssen Betrayed America, 2002.
Tiger Trap: America's Secret Spy War with China, 2011.

Further Reading

Schudel, Matt. "David Wise, Author and CIA Expert Who Exposed 'invisible government,' Dies at 88." *Washington Post* (9 Oct. 2018).

Seelye, Katharine Q. "David Wise, Journalist Who Exposed Covert C.I.A. Activity, Is Dead at 88." *The New York Times* (10 Oct. 2018).

Wise, David. *Contemporary Authors*. Vols. 1–4, 1st Rev. Detroit: Gale Research, 1967.

Wise, David. *Contemporary Authors, New Revision Series*. Vol. 42. Detroit: Gale Research, 1994.

Wise, David. *Contemporary Authors, New Revision Series*. Detroit: Gale, Cengage Learning, 2012.

Wise, David, and S. E. Kramer. "My Life in the Shadows." *Best Life* 5.2 (Mar. 2000).

Bob Woodward (1943–)

Bob Woodward and Carl Bernstein uncovered a series of events that angered and then indirectly forced President Richard Nixon from office.

Woodward was born on March 26, 1943, in Geneva, Illinois. Upon his graduation from high school in 1961, he entered Yale University on a naval ROTC scholarship. When he received his degree in 1965, he fulfilled his obligation to the United States Navy by serving as a communications officer aboard two ships and as a communications liaison officer in Washington, D. C.

After he completed five years of duty, he applied to the law school at Harvard. Although he was accepted, he decided to become a reporter instead. He tried *The Washington Post*, where for two weeks he wrote stories that were not published. The editors of the newspaper advised him to return when he had some journalistic experience and helped him obtain a job with the *Montgomery County Sentinel*. There, he was assigned civic association meetings and press releases. Woodward emphatically hated the work. Within weeks he was covering stories in his off-hours. If the topics were interesting, the *Sentinel* used them.

Woodward returned to *The Washington Post* in 1971 and became an investigative reporter. Although he was not considered the newspaper's best writer, he was energetic and persistent, and his stories on drugs, police corruption, restaurants, business corruption, Blue Cross-Blue Shield, and Medicaid abuses made the front pages. In short, he would follow a tip or lead until the end.

In 1972 Barry Sussman, the newspaper's city editor, called Woodward and informed him that five well-dressed men had been arrested for burglarizing the Democratic National Committee's headquarters in the Watergate complex. Woodward attended the arraignment and subsequently helped write a front-page story on the break-in. Story after story appeared, each disclosing another link between the burglars and the White House.

Woodward had been assigned to cover the burglary and had written several other stories concerning Watergate, but Carl Bernstein, another *Post* reporter, realized that Woodward could not cover all the tips and leads, and persuaded the editors to allow him to cover the subject, too. Within four months "Woodstein" had traced the money to Attorney General John Mitchell, the campaign director of CREEP (Committee to Re-Elect the President) at the time of the break-in.

In 1974 the reporters' *All the President's Men*, which was meant to be the culmination of their tedious, meticulous work until other major reporters began investigating Watergate, was published. The book, which disclosed how the authors investigated the various leads, including successes as well as failures in obtaining information for stories, was written from the third-person point of view for the sake of objectivity. It was praised by critics for its realistic depiction of the newspaper business and its authentic record of history.

Two years later the reporters' *The Final Days* appeared. Woodward and Bernstein had intended to write about the impeachment and subsequent trial of the president from the perspective of six senators involved in the case, but when they learned that Nixon would resign the idea was dismissed. Woodward and Bernstein received a year's leave of absence and began investigating the last fifteen months of the Nixon White House. After interviewing almost 400 persons, they wrote an in-depth account of the last days. The book sold well, but several critics, including James J. Kilpatrick and William Safire, lambasted the book for its disregard of historical reporting. The scenes of the president with Henry Kissinger were considered by some critics to be unnecessary. Other critics termed the book a nonfiction novel because of its style and anonymous sources. Most reviewers considered it an extraordinary piece of contemporary history.

Woodward returned to the newspaper, but Bernstein resigned to devote his time to freelance writing. In 1979 Woodward became an editor at the newspaper. The same year, with Scott Armstrong, he wrote *The Brethren: Inside the Supreme Court*, which examined the Supreme Court justices during the years 1969 to 1976 and specific cases such as *Moore v. Illinois*. Although the authors claimed they had access to several justices and at least 170 law clerks, some critics complained that no source was mentioned by name and that so-called facts were incorrect.

In 1981 Woodward became an assistant managing editor at the newspaper.

The following year he was asked by John Belushi's widow, Judy Jacklin Belushi, to write about her husband's death. Woodward interviewed numerous individuals and wrote a stark account of Belushi's death from drugs titled *Wired: The Short Life and Fast Times of John Belushi*, which was published in 1984. Woodward was criticized for focusing on the comedian's dark side, particularly on the drugs and alcohol that ultimately destroyed his life. Even Belushi's widow complained about the book's negative perspective.

In 1987 Woodward wrote *Veil: The Secret Wars of the CIA, 1981–1987*, which concerned the late William Casey, the former director of the Central Intelligence Agency (CIA), and the agency's covert operations during President Ronald Reagan's administration. Indeed, the book chronicled

Casey's six-year tenure as the nation's chief intelligence officer, which ended with his resignation and death in 1987. Woodward disclosed the agency's attempted assassination of Sheikh Mohammed Hussein Fadlallah, who led the militant Lebanese Shi'ite faction known as Hizbollah. The car bombing killed eighty people, but Fadlallah was unharmed. Woodward was criticized for not identifying sources. He claimed he had interviewed Casey numerous times before his death, but Casey's family, including his widow, refuted this claim.

Woodward examined President George H. W. Bush's administration, especially the policies pertaining to the invasion of Panama and the war in the Persian Gulf, in *The Commanders*, which was published in 1991. Woodward claimed he had interviewed more than 400 individuals for the book. However, not one of them was cited. Woodward confirmed that Bush was responsible for the policy in the Gulf. He also revealed that Colin Powell was a leader who respected those who used restraint.

In 1994 Woodward examined the White House under the Clinton administration in *The Agenda: Inside the Clinton White House*. The book focused on Clinton's first year as president, providing a behind-the-scenes glance at his presidency, including the pluses and the minuses.

The Choice: How Bill Clinton Won was published in 1996 and concerned the political race between President Clinton and Senator Bob Dole, the Republican challenger. Critics claimed readers learned more about Bob Dole and his wife than they did about Bill Clinton and his wife.

In 1999 Woodward's book *Shadow: Five Presidents and the Legacy of Watergate* was published. Woodward examined Watergate and its impact on the presidents who followed Nixon: Gerald Ford, Jimmy Carter, Ronald Reagan, George H. W. Bush, and Bill Clinton. Critics pointed out that Woodward used direct quotations that may or may not have been said.

Maestro: Greenspan's Fed and the American Boom was published in 2000. This book concerned Alan Greenspan, perhaps the most successful chairman of the Federal Reserve. Indeed, the nation's economy under Greenspan was mostly sound and healthy.

The first book concerning President George W. Bush and his administration was *Bush at War*, which was published in 2002 and which concerned the war in Afghanistan after the terrorists attacked the United States on September 11, 2001. Two years later *Plan of Attack* was published and concerned President George W. Bush's plan to start a war against Saddam Hussein and Iraq. Overall, critics believed the book suffered from the author's writing, too many facts, and not enough analysis.

In 2006 *State of Denial* was published. In this book Woodward chronicled President George W. Bush and his administration's mismanagement of the war in Iraq. Critics claimed Woodward presented a picture of the president as being uninformed and not necessarily intelligent. They claimed he depicted the secretary of defense as someone who lacked military knowledge such as strategy or tactics.

The War Within: A Secret White House History (2006–2008) was published in 2008 and concerned President George W. Bush and his administration's new war strategy in Iraq, which called for an additional 30,000 soldiers and which caused considerable tension and disagreement among members of the president's administration.

Woodward examined President Barack Obama and his administration in *Obama's War*, which was published in 2010. The book specifically looked at President Obama's decisions regarding terrorism and the war in Afghanistan and Iraq. Although President Obama desired to end the war, his military advisors were not necessarily on board. The book also revealed how unprepared the government was if terrorists exploded a nuclear bomb somewhere in the United States.

The Price of Politics, which was published in 2012, examined the debt ceiling crisis of 2011 and President Obama's relationship with the Republicans, particularly Speaker of the House John Boehner, and Democrats in the Capitol building. Like too many of his previous books, several critics claimed this book merely scratched the surface by providing facts and not enough analysis.

In 2015 *The Last of the President's Men* was published. The book focused on Alexander Butterfield, the former aide to President Richard Nixon who was responsible for the secret taping system in the White House. The book was based on numerous interviews with Butterfield as well as twenty boxes of files and documents. As a result, the reader learned about Butterfield and his professional relationship with the president.

The first book about President Trump and his administration, *Fear: Trump in the White House*, was published in 2018 and revealed the decision- making process by President Trump and members of his administration. The book depicted the Trump White House as being chaotic, to say the least. Of course, Woodward did not discuss at length all the accusations that were thrown at the president by the Democrats. Nor did he discuss at length the various investigations of the president that were initiated by the Democrats. In short, as more than one critic pointed out, the book was not objective in its depiction of the subject.

Rage was published in 2020 and was similar to *Fear* in tone. In short, the book examined the decision-making process by President Trump and members of his administration regarding national security, racial unrest, and the weak economy caused by the pandemic.

In 2021 Woodward and Robert Costa published *Peril*, which concerned the Trump White House, the 2020 presidential campaign, and the Biden White House.

Although Woodward has received numerous awards for his work over the years, he has made a few mistakes while working at the *Post*. For instance, in 1980 he supported Janet Cooke's story about an eight-year-old addict, which was published in the newspaper. Later, it was revealed the story was not based on an actual child. Woodward, like others at the newspaper, was not aware of this fact. Several critics claimed the story was nothing but fiction.

Representative Works

All the President's Men (with Carl Bernstein), 1974.
The Final Days (with Carl Bernstein), 1976.
The Brethren: Inside the Supreme Court (with Scott Armstrong), 1979.
Veil: The Secret Wars of the CIA, 1981–1987, 1987.
The Commanders, 1991.
The Agenda: Inside the Clinton White House, 1994.
The Choice: How Bill Clinton Won, 1996.
Shadow: Five Presidents and the Legacy of Watergate, 1999.
Bush at War, 2002.
Plan of Attack, 2004.
State of Denial, 2006.
The War Within: A Secret White House History (2006–2008), 2008.
Obama's War, 2010.
The Price of Politics, 2012.
Fear: Trump in the White House, 2018.
Rage, 2020.
Peril (with Robert Costa), 2021.

Further Reading

Adrian Havill. *Deep Truth: The Lives of Bob Woodward and Carl Bernstein*. Secaucus, NJ: Carol Publishing Group, 1993.
"Bob Woodward." *Gale Literature: Contemporary Authors*. Gale, 2019.
"Bob Woodward." The Academy of Achievement. achievement.org/achiever/bob-woodward.

SELECTED BIBLIOGRAPHY

In addition to the resources at the end of each biographical entry, the following works may be helpful to readers who desire to learn more about investigative journalism and its practitioners.

Aucoin, James. *The Evolution of American Investigative Journalism*. Columbia: University of Missouri Press, 2006.

Beasley, Maurine H., and Sheila Gibbons. *Taking Their Place: A Documentary History of Women and Journalism*. Lanham, MD.: University Press of America, 1993.

Behrens, John C. *The Typewriter Guerrillas: Closeups of 20 Top Investigative Reporters*. Chicago: Nelson-Hall, 1977.

Belford, Barbara. *Brilliant Bylines: A Biographical Anthology of Notable Newspaperwomen in America*. New York: Columbia University Press, 1986.

Black, Jeremy. *The English Press in the Eighteenth Century*. Philadelphia: University of Pennsylvania Press, 1987.

Bleyer, Willard Grosvenor. *Main Currents in the History of American Journalism*. Boston: Houghton Mifflin, 1927.

Brasch, Walter M. *Forerunners of Revolution: Muckrakers and the American Social Conscience*. Lanham, MD.: University Press of America, 1990.

Brendon, Piers. *The Life and Death of the Press Barons*. New York: Atheneum, 1983.

Bulman, David, ed. *Molders of Opinion*. Milwaukee: Bruce, 1945.

Chalmers, David Mark. *The Social and Political Ideas of the Muckrakers*. New York: Citadel, 1964.

Chalmers, David Mark. *The Muckrake Years*. New York: D. Van Nostrand Co., 1974.

Cook, Fred J. *The Muckrakers: Crusading Journalists Who Changed America*. New York: Doubleday, 1972.

Daly, Christopher B. *Covering America: A Narrative History of a Nation's Journalism*. Amherst and Boston: University of Massachusetts Press, 2012.

Davidson, Philip. *Propaganda and the American Revolution, 1763–1783*. Chapel Hill: University of North Carolina Press, 1941.

Dennis, Everette E., and William L. Rivers. *Other Voices: The New Journalism in America*. San Francisco: Canfield, 1974.

Downie, Leonard. *The New Muckrakers*. Washington: New Republic Books, 1976.

Drewry, John E., ed. *Post Biographies of Famous Journalists*. Athens: University of Georgia Press, 1942.

Dygert, James H. *The Investigative Journalist: Folk Heroes of a New Era*. Englewood Cliffs, N.J.: Prentice-Hall, 1976.

Ettema, James S., and Theodore L. Glasser. *Custodians of Conscience: Investigative Journalism and Public Virtue*. New York: Columbia University Press, 1998.

Filler, Louis. *Crusaders for American Liberalism*. New York: Harcourt, Brace and Co., 1932.

Filler, Louis. *The Muckrakers*. University Park: Pennsylvania State University Press, 1976.

Ford, Edwin H., and Edwin Emery, eds. *Highlights in the History of the American Press: A Book of Readings*. Minneapolis: University of Minnesota Press, 1954.

Frank, Joseph. *The Beginnings of the English Newspaper: 1620–1660*. Cambridge, MA: Harvard University Press, 1961.

Graham, Otis L., Jr. *An Encore for Reform: The Old Progressives and the New Deal*. New York: Oxford University Press, 1967.

Greenwald, Marilyn S., and Joseph Bernt, eds. *The Big Chill: Investigative Reporting in the Current Media Environment*. Ames: Iowa State University Press, 2000.

Hallin, Daniel C. *The "Uncensored War": The Media and Vietnam*. New York: Oxford University Press, 1986.

Harrison, John and Harry Stein, eds. *Muckraking: Past, Present and Future*. University Park: Pennsylvania State University Press, 1973.

Hart, Jim Allee. *Views on the News: The Developing Editorial Syndrome, 1500–1800*. Carbondale: Southern Illinois University Press, 1970.

Heald, Morrell. *Transatlantic Vistas: American Journalists in Europe 1900–1940*. Kent, Ohio: Kent State University Press, 1988.

Hofstadter, Richard. *The Age of Reform: From Bryan to F.D.R*. New York: Alfred A. Knopf, 1955.

Hudson, Frederic. *Journalism in the United States, from 1690–1872*. New York: Harper, 1873.

Hynds, Ernest C. *American Newspapers in the 1980s*. New York: Hastings House, 1980.

Jensen, Carl. *Stories That Changed America: Muckrakers of the 20th Century*. New York: Seven Stories Press, 2000.

Kessler, Lauren. *The Dissident Press: Alternative Journalism in American History*. Beverly Hills, CA: Sage, 1984.

Kobre, Sidney. *Development of American Journalism*. Dubuque, Iowa: Brown, 1969.

Littlefield, Roy Everett. *William Randolph Hearst: His Role in American Progressivism*. Lanham, MD: University Press of America, 1980.

MacDougall, Curtis D. *Interpretative Reporting*. New York: Macmillan, 1977.

Marzolf, Martion. *Up from the Footnote: A History of Women Journalists*. New York: Hastings House, 1977.

Miraldi, Robert, ed. *The Muckrakers: Evangelical Crusaders*. Westport, CT: Praeger, 2000.

Miraldi, Robert. *Muckraking and Objectivity: Journalism's Colliding Traditions*. Westport, CT: Greenwood Press, 1990.

Mott, Frank Luther. *A History of American Magazines, Vol. IV: 1885–1905*. Cambridge, MA: Belknap Press, 1957.

Mott, Frank Luther. *American Journalism: A History, 1690–1960*. New York: Macmillan, 1962.

Payne, George Henry. *History of Journalism in the United States*. New York: Appleton-Century-Crofts, 1920.

Peterson, Theodore. *Magazines in the Twentieth Century*. Urbana: University of Illinois Press, 1964.

Pickett, Calder M. *Voices of the Past: Key Documents in the History of American Journalism*. Columbus, Ohio: Grid, 1977.

Pilger, John, ed. *Tell Me No Lies: Investigative Journalism and Its Triumphs*. New York: Random House, 2011; originally 2004.

Protess, David L., Fay Lomax Cook, Jack C. Doppelt, James S. Ettema, Margaret T. Gordon, Donna R. Leff, and Peter Miller. *The Journalism of Outrage: Investigative Reporting and Agenda Building in America*. New York: Guilford, 1991.

Regier, C. C. *The Era of the Muckrakers*. Gloucester, MA: Peter Smith, 1957; originally 1932.

Ross, Ishbell. *Ladies of the Press: The Story of Women in Journalism by an Insider*. New York: Harper and Brothers, 1936.

Schiffron, Anya, ed. *Global Muckraking: 100 Years of Investigative Journalism from Around the World*. New York: The New Press, 2014.

Schilpp, Madelon Golden, and Sharon M. Murphy. *Great Women of the Press*. Carbondale: Southern Illinois University Press, 1983.

Schneirov, Matthew. *The Dream of a New Social Order: Popular Magazines in America, 1893–1914*. New York: Columbia University Press, 1994.

Schudson, Michael. *Discovering the News*. New York: Basic Books, 1978.

Serrin, Judith and William, eds. *Muckraking! The Journalism that Changed America*. New York: New Press, 2002.

Shapiro, Bruce, ed. *Shaking the Foundations: 200 Years of Investigative Journalism in America*. New York: Thunder's Mouth Press/Nation Books, 2003.

Shapiro, Herbert, ed. *The Muckrakers and American Society*. Boston: D. C. Heath, 1968.

Sloan, William David, and Julie Hedgepeth Williams. *The Early American Press, 1690–1783*, History of American Journalism Series. Westport, CT: Greenwood Press, 1994.

Stevens, John D. *Sensationalism and the New York Press*. New York: Columbia University Press, 1991.

Tassin, Algernon. *The Magazine in America*. New York: Dodd, Mead and Co., 1916.

Tebbel, John, and Mary Ellen Zuckerman. *The Magazine in America: 1741–1990*. New York: Oxford University Press, 1991.

Villard, Oswald Garrison. *Some Newspapers and Newspaper-Men*. New York: Knopf, 1923.

Weinberg, Arthur and Lila, eds. *The Muckrakers*. New York: Simon and Schuster, 1961.

Wilson, Harold S. *McClure's Magazine and the Muckrakers*. Princeton, N.J.: Princeton University Press, 1970.

Wood, James Playsted. *Magazines in the United States*. New York: Ronald Press, 1956.

INDEX

A

B

C

D

E

F

G

H

L

M

O

P

Q

R

S

Y

Z

ABOUT THE AUTHOR

Professor Emeritus Edd Applegate received his doctorate from Oklahoma State University and taught undergraduate and graduate courses in advertising and mass communications primarily at Middle Tennessee State University until he retired several years ago. In addition to teaching, he contributed chapters and entries to scholarly books and encyclopedias, articles to refereed academic journals and national conferences, and wrote books for academic and reference publishers.

Made in the USA
Las Vegas, NV
19 September 2026

6e9526e2-fb16-4006-a598-40a33019011bR01